# The Mystery of B. Traven

# The Mystery of
# B. Traven

Judy Stone

William Kaufmann, Inc.    Los Altos, California

# TO THE BEACHCOMBER

**Library of Congress Cataloging in Publication Data**
Stone, Judy, 1924-
    The Mystery of B. Traven.

    Bibliography: p.
    1. Traven, B.—Biography.  2. Traven, B.—Interviews.
3. Authors, Mexican—20th century—Biography.
4. Authors, German—20th century—Biography.
I. Title
PT3919.T7Z89     813'.5'2  [B]     76-54942
ISBN 0-913232-32-7

ACKNOWLEDGMENTS: Warren Hinckle, editor of the now defunct *Ramparts* magazine, had the imagination to see how the story of B. Traven and his works would appeal to a new generation. Carolyn Sammet offered friendship and hospitality in Mexico; without them, this project might never have been completed. Alvah Bessie had the answer to my question "What do you know about B. Traven?" that led to the late Philip Stevenson, screenwriter of *Rosa Blanca*. Stevenson let me use his name to pave the way when I wrote my first letter to "Hal Croves." Soñora Babb Howe shared memories of her good friend, Esperanza Lopez Mateos, and recollections of the first worm-eaten manuscripts she saw by B. Traven. Henry Dietrich, a Traven enthusiast with first editions in German, never seemed bored by the problems I brought to him. Brigitte Powell, Federico Benemann, and Catherine Byrne translated, but Catherine helped boost my sagging morale as well. The Hoover Institution, Stanford University, had a complete file of *Der Ziegelbrenner*—plus an odd one published in 1930 that did not come from the hand of Ret Marut/B. Traven. Gabriel Figueroa was unfailingly courteous, kind, and helpful. Albert Maltz shared his knowledge of Traven. Bernard Smith graciously discussed the editing problems he had when Traven's works were being prepared for publication by Alfred A. Knopf. The late Oskar Maria Graf put me in touch with Rolf Recknagel. Recknagel's book was invaluable for my own work. Two friends, now dead, gave help and support: my agent Cyrilly Abels and Ethel Duffy Turner, an old California anarchist who loved Mexico and the works of B. T. Arthur Wang and Larry Hill offered early encouragement. My brothers, Izzy, Marc and Lou, tough critics and loving supporters, always. Rosa Elena Luján never failed to be gracious under the most trying circumstances. Most of all, my appreciation to B. T. for his example of integrity, for the books he wrote, and for his kindness to this journalist, despite everything.

# Contents

# Introduction

Where shall I begin to tell my story about B. Traven? With the sardonic writer who can draw his reader tenderly into the heart of a Mexican peasant, the writer known mainly in the United States for *The Treasure of the Sierra Madre?* Shall I start with a deaf old man on a sunlit patio in Mexico City in 1967 stubbornly clinging to his secrets? Or with a brave young revolutionary editor facing execution on May Day 1919, in Munich, Germany, a country ripped apart by war, rebellion, murder, treachery and despair?

Traven's identity is a mystery that for 40 years has teased millions of his readers throughout the world. It is a story so complicated by life and so obscured by design that it would take an international team of detectives to unravel all the threads, and a novelist greater than Traven to plumb the tragedy, the pain, the loneliness, the gamesmanship, the love and the irony in the true story of this writer for whom irony is the spice of life.

"You ought to have some papers to show who you are," the police officer advised the sailor without a passport in B. Traven's novel *The Death Ship.* "I don't need any paper; I know who I am," he said.

B. Traven knew who he was. Perhaps. He played so many roles and when he was old and tired he was bedeviled still. People kept demanding, "*Why* don't you tell us who you are?"

He was all these people:

Ret Marut, actor and editor, registered as an alien by Dusseldorf police in 1912. Birthplace: San Francisco, on February 25, 1882. Nationality: English, later mysteriously changed to American.

Richard Maurhut, German novelist.

Berick Traven Torsvan, who said he was born in Chicago, Illinois, on May 3, 1890, finally a citizen of Mexico under that name.

Hal Croves, Traven's "agent" and scriptwriter.

1

How many other pseudonyms and false papers for one man, haunted forever by the question of his birth, crying out, "I do not want to be anything but a human being, a man"? How terrible for life to force deceptions upon an honest man.

Although I had admired B. Traven's novels, *The Death Ship* and *The Rebellion of the Hanged,* for many years, I did not become curious about the author until 1964. At that time, during a Christmas vacation in Mexico City, I tried to learn what had happened to a Mexican movie based on Traven's novel *Rosa Blanca* (The White Rose) about the maneuvers of an American oil magnate to grab Mexican land for exploitation. It was filmed in 1962 and not released until after his death on March 26, 1969. Its quiet disappearance was a mystery replete with the smell of oil and international politics. In 1966, I was rewarded—and frustrated—by an unprecedented series of interviews with Traven, "the man who never gives interviews." They were interviews which raised more questions than they answered. The questions multiplied while I spent maddening months working with German translators on Ret Marut's vitriolic anti-war newspaper *Der Ziegelbrenner* (The Brickburner) and a whole world opened up that I had known nothing about.

The history books can spare only a few lines for the Bavarian Revolution because what followed required volumes. But the history of our time might have been different if that revolution had succeeded, a revolution led by a handful of Jewish writers—Social Democrats, anarchists, Communists, Utopians: they believed in Germany and humanity. Their revolution was born without bloodshed on November 7, 1918, and died May 1, 1919, in the agony of 600 murders, the first casualties of World War II. Who can blame the man who wanted to forget that he ever took part in the life and death of that country? He chose to maintain absolute silence about that period of his life.

I felt unhappily like an interloper when I first met Traven in May 1966, and I felt unhappily that way while writing about him. He tried so hard for so long to defend his privacy. I would like to have left him in peace. I would like to have forgotten the whole thing—all the confusion and contradictions in Traven's life—but that history kept nagging at me. When I tried to forget it by turning to the daily paper, I fell prey to history's troubling analogies.

In that echo from Bavaria, there were not only parallels to political events here, but also to attitudes. There was not much distance in space or time between the hippies' plea: "Make love not war" and Ret Marut, writing angrily in flight from Germany in 1921:

"To be ashamed to look like a tramp is the right of the bourgeoisie. To have this right to be taken for a wealthy citizen makes you into a slave ... If you could put everything into your own bag, then the cannons would rust and the walls of the citadel would fall ... "

A whole new generation that would respond to Traven's anarchistic approach to life and his undoctrinaire rebelliousness doesn't even know his name. Although Traven's 12 novels have appeared in more than 500 editions in 36 languages and have sold in the millions of copies in Europe and Latin America, only five had been published in the United States up to 1967 and most of them were out of print. His writing may seem occasionally old-fashioned or awkward, but his storytelling is superb and his powerful, ironic foresight shows a contemporary 20th century vision. Kenneth Rexroth, discussing *Disengagement: The Art of the Beat Generation* in 1957, said: "The first and still the greatest novelist of total disengagement is not a young man at all, but an elderly IWW of German ancestry, B. Traven ... "

When "Hal Croves" invited me to his home in Mexico, I had assumed that he was willing to talk about the past, Traven's past. Señora Rosa Elena Luján, officially known as Traven's "agent," a handsome, black-eyed woman then in her fifties, picked me up at the hotel, introduced herself as "Mrs. Croves" and drove me to their home on a modest side street off Mexico City's beautiful tree-lined boulevard, the Reforma. Croves walked slowly out to the patio to greet me. He was slightly under medium height, with whitish hair worn long and an imperious-looking nose that dominated his face. Although he was sportily dressed with an ascot tucked neatly into his jacket, he appeared frail and helpless because his hearing aid was not working properly, querulous because a new battery had not been purchased for it, and a sense of his agitation on meeting a stranger, a reporter, filled the air. Behind the thick glasses of a scholar, his blue eyes, magnified, looked sad and lost in some other world of his own. His deafness added a strange dimension to our meeting. It seemed an insurmountable obstacle obliterating even the possibility of easily asking the questions I knew he would be reluctant to answer.

Suddenly he began to speak in a rush of words, his English accented by a trace of German. "Forget the man!" he cried in passion. "What does it matter if he is the son of a Hohenzollern prince or anyone else? Write about his works. Write how he is against anything which is forced upon human beings, including communism or Bolshevism. See how, among all of Traven's books, there goes one thought like a red thread from the first line of his first book to the last line of his last book. Since he doesn't want to be a reformer or preacher, he lets the reader get the red thread."

That thread began to unwind for me as I read his other books and listened to him expound on the philosophy behind Traven's works—only the philosophy, never the person. But I didn't begin to understand him or the motivation behind his writing until I studied his newspaper, *Der Ziegelbrenner,* and went back into history to learn about the Bavarian Revolution. All that followed reflected those days of hope and shattered illusions, and it is there that the story of B. Traven began.

# Part One: The "Unknown" German Revolution

... Yet who is he that could stand a hundred questions and answer none? An unanswered question flutters about you for the rest of your life. It does not let you sleep; it does not let you think. You feel that the equilibrium of the universe is at stake if you leave a question pending. A question without an answer is something so incomplete that you simply cannot bear it. You can get crazy thinking of the problems of an unbalanced solar system. The word "why" with a question mark behind it is the cause, I am quite certain, of all culture, civilization, progress, and science. This word "why" has changed and will again change every system by which mankind lives and prospers; it will end war, and it will bring war again; it will lead to communism, and it will surely destroy communism again; it will make dictators and despots, and it will dethrone them again; it will make new religions, and it will turn them into superstitions again; it will make a nebula the real and spiritual center of the universe, and it will again make the same nebula an insignificant speck in the super-universe. The little word "why" with a question mark. — *The Death Ship* by B. Traven

# 1 A War Ends; a Revolution Dies; the German Right Begins Its Rise to Power

Springtime in Munich, 1919; the stench of death filled the air, the streets and jails were clogged with the dead and the wounded, defeat and starvation dogged the people, but in the beer gardens, the regimental bands of Germany's new Social Democratic Republic blared out the national anthem, "Deutschland über Alles." The threat of Bolshevism had been destroyed: Bavaria's infant Soviet Republic was dead. In the 19th Infantry barracks, White guards, government troops from Berlin, wearing white armbands, shot at random every tenth soldier, a lesson to those who might have been sympathetic to the Soldiers' and Workers' Councils that had sprung up in the wake of the Armistice. One soldier was to be spared; his snappy salutes in the midst of a rebellious, disintegrating Army had brought him to the attention of Reichswehr officers. They had fled revolutionary Munich, leaving that one man behind to spy on his fellow soldiers. He was punctilious about his first political task and delivered his reports in writing. "His indictments," wrote one of his friends, "cast a merciless clarity upon the unspeakable disgrace of the military treason practiced by the Jewish dictatorship of Munich's Soviet period." The soldier-informer was Adolf Hitler.

For more than a year, revolution had erupted through Europe. On March 15, 1917, Czar Nicholas abdicated; on November 7, 1917, the Bolsheviks overthrew the Kerensky provisional government; the Hapsburg dynasty fell in Vienna; on November 7, 1918, Kurt Eisner, an Independent (left) Social Democrat from Berlin, proclaimed the end of the royal Wittelsbach rule in Bavaria and announced the formation of the Bavarian Republic. In the tradition of German law and order, Eisner instructed "all bureaucrats to remain at their posts"—a tragicomic notice considering the internecine warfare among splinter factions of Social Democrats, anarchists, just plain bohemians, and pro-Bolshevik Spartacists.

7

In Berlin, on November 9, a reluctant Social Democratic Party took over the new Republic of Germany and Kaiser Wilhelm II fled to Holland. On the very day of the foundation of the German Republic, a secret agreement took place which was to prove its death blow: Friedrich Ebert, a leader of the majority Social Democrats, made a pact with General Wilhelm Groener, second in command of the Germany Army. Ebert, who once said he hated revolution "like sin," promised to "put down anarchy and Bolshevism and maintain the Army in all its traditions," and the general pledged the Army's support—a pledge he was finally unable to carry out—to help the new government establish itself. But the conflict between the Army with its Prussian traditions and the anti-militarist Socialists soon came to a head. In December, the first Soviet Congress of Germany demanded the dismissal of Field Marshal von Hindenburg and the abolition of the Regular Army; the Army in turn demanded action against the Spartacists headed by Karl Liebknecht and Rosa Luxemburg. Two days after Christmas, Ebert, provisional head of the government, appointed Gustav Noske minister of national defense. Noske, a former master butcher who was quite pleased with his role as "bloodhound," crushed the Spartacists in Berlin, and Spartacist leaders Luxemburg and Liebknecht were captured and murdered on January 15. These were the first of a long series of political assassinations that went basically unpunished along the road that led to Auschwitz.

On February 21, Eisner was killed in Munich by a right-wing officer, Count Anton Arco-Valley, a half-Jew who had been refused admission to the conspiratorial and racist Thule Society led by Rudolf Hess and Dietrich Eckart. The Bavarians rallied behind Eisner as they had never done when he was alive, and two crazily confused Soviet Republics were set up. But on May 1, 1919, Regular Army troops from Berlin and Bavarian "free corps" volunteers overthrew the government and massacred hundreds, radicals and non-radicals alike. From this bloody soil the German right flourished, and from this Bavarian base Adolf Hitler rose to power.

# 2 Enter Ret Marut, of Uncertain Parentage, Who Publishes an Anti-War, Anti-Capitalist Magazine in the Thick of World War I

Among those arrested on May 1 was a young man known as Ret Marut. Slight and quiet, apparently about 37 years old, he had been a minor actor and director in German theaters from 1906 to 1915. In 1917, he appeared in Munich and began publishing *Der Ziegelbrenner,* a small, booklet-like magazine with a brick-red cover that, like its title, proclaimed his intention to lay a foundation for a better world. The magazine was filled with passionate attacks against militarism, nationalism, materialism, religious hypocrisy and a venal press. There were lyrical translations from Shelley and a constant invocation of Goethe as the great, true spirit of Germany. There are a few glimpses of the editor's tender, angry heart behind his resolutely ironic vision, as well as an occasional petty vindictiveness in shoddy contrast to his great insight—qualities to be found later in the novels that were to make him famous under the name of B. Traven.

Marut was a lonely and eccentric figure, but it was a lonely time for a man of conviction. In every country, there were few Socialists and pacifists who had maintained the courage of their convictions with the call to arms in 1914. In Germany, 93 of the most noted artists, scientists and philosophers issued a "Manifesto to the Civilized World" in October 1914, denying German violations of Belgian neutrality and stories of German atrocities. The Manifesto spoke of the "shameful spectacle . . . of Russian hordes . . . allied with Mongols and Negroes . . . unleashed against the white race" and declared that German *Kultur* would have been wiped off the face of the earth had it not been for German militarism. Only a few individuals were willing to go on public record challenging this *Kulturwelt* Manifesto. One was Albert Einstein.

Another figure in Germany's minority intellectual opposition was the man known as Marut, who, in Munich, set about condemning war and nationalism in his own highly individualistic, subscribers-be-damned attitude. In the early issues of the sporadically published

*Der Ziegelbrenner,* he expressed a kind of love for the potentiality of German spiritual leadership, but by 1921, it was transformed into a cry of anguish and contempt: "If only I could be a foreigner who wouldn't have any blood relationship with the new Germany," he wrote in one of his last issues, published while the writer was in flight from Germany, shortly thereafter to disappear forever as Marut and begin to write as B. Traven.

Marut's "blood relationship" to Germany is obscure. One theory about the name—Marut was one of the first in a long series of pseudonyms—was developed by Rolf Recknagel, of the School of Librarianship in Leipzig in East Germany. He spent ten painstaking years comparing the works of Marut, the obscure German polemicist and the famous—but mysterious—Traven. Recknagel's book *B. Traven: Beiträge zur Biografie* (B. Traven: Materials for a Biography), published in 1966, provided massive documentation linking the two. Marut is the Indo-Aryan word for storm clouds (a similar name, Gales, was later used for the first person narrator in several of Traven's novels). In the Rigveda, the most ancient (2000-1000 B.C.) hymns of the Hindus, the storm clouds "assume the defiant name of the Maruts . . . fierce in strength . . . these Maruts have brought together heaven and earth . . . who are these resplendent men? . . . No one indeed knows their births; they alone know each other's birthplace. . . . These Maruts stir up even the sluggard, even the vagrant, as the gods pleased. O strong ones, drive away the darkness, and grant us all our kith and kin."*

In a routine police registration for aliens in Dusseldorf in 1912, Marut said he was born on February 25, 1882, in San Francisco. He gave England as his homeland, but on August 1, 1914, the day Kaiser Wilhelm II decreed a general mobilization, Marut had England—a potential enemy—changed to America, a switch that even today mystifies German police. Who authorized such an essential change? A Munich police warrant for Marut's arrest in 1919 listed both parents as dead; his father's name was given as William and his mother's maiden name as Helene Ottarent. Marut informed police that he was an impresario from San Francisco. He had once told his close friend,

---

* The interest in Hindu literature which, along with LSD, became part of the so-called "psychedelic" movement in the USA, became fashionable in Germany after the Upanishads captured Schopenhauer's imagination. Sanskrit departments were established in nearly all of the German universities about the turn of the century, and plays from the Sanskrit were produced on German stages.

Elfriede Zielke, an actress, that his mother was Irish, his father English, and that he himself had been born on a ship, his birth papers deposited in San Francisco, and the records destroyed in the 1906 fire and earthquake.

It is interesting that an issue of *Der Ziegelbrenner* carried a similar story—an excerpt from *Denied a Country* by the Danish novelist Herman Bang: "Joán heard Jens Lund saying to Collyett: 'Melbourne, Melbourne, country—country: It makes me wild to hear all this talk about one's country. Why do you suppose I am greater than anybody else? Because I have no country . . . Country? My parents were more obliging. They didn't give me one. The man without a country is a free man, and I was born on the high seas which connect all countries. One's country—what is it? Trotting around the same table and keeping our thumb in the same groove that our forefathers' thumbs have scooped out. I *have* a country, and that, sir, is called *Myself*. There I am king and people and parliament and lawgiver. *I* am my country and *I* am its government . . .' "

The man without a country, or proof of nationality, later became Traven's central theme in *The Death Ship*. A preoccupation with birth records, illegitimacy and official documents is the most important element in the novelist's strained and confounding attempts to hide his true identity—a preoccupation reflected constantly in his writings as Marut, and as Traven.

Although San Francisco's city records were destroyed in the 1906 fire, the San Francisco Chronicle's birth announcements for February 25, 1882, show none of the names used by Marut. Although Traven presumably knew where he was born and grew up, his "earliest childhood dreams" were about Germany. In *Der Ziegelbrenner,* he wrote of his "strong longing" for Germany, a longing that could only be understood "by one who experiences like me that one's homeland is not a piece of earth but an idea, an idea which might be expressed as 'belonging to a certain specific world of culture and thought that finds its visual expression in the language.' "

He passionately wanted Germany to live up to his idealized dreams. When the first issue of *Der Ziegelbrenner* was published on September 1, 1917, Germany appeared to be winning the war on the eastern front. But Marut pointed out that anyone who had lived abroad, as he had, knew that Germany's spiritual influence upon the rest of the world was not as great as Germans thought. England and America knew as much about Germany as they did about Serbia and evaluated its people in about the same way: "half-barbaric and choleric."

Although a new image of Germany was emerging, Marut warned that eventual victory would lie, not in conquests, but in Germany's ability to rise to the heights demanded of a world leader.

Marut urged his readers "to understand that the only cause of this mass disaster is money . . . It was capitalism which suggested to mankind that the highest goal in life is the acquisition of money. . . . Only in this way is it understandable that England is conducting the war to make business more profitable and that Germany is conducting the war to safeguard and support her always steadily increasing volume of business. You can turn that over at will but from all pores of this war there exudes the concept of money. Even the ideals fought for are in the last analysis only money concepts made magical."

He explained that people who lead drab lives have a need to participate in the excitement of war. If men and women could fulfill all their potentialities in stimulating and constructive work, no country in the world would succeed in drumming up an aggressive, martial spirit, he predicted.

Marut called for "a totally new construction of our thinking. . . ." He declared that "it must be made impossible . . . for hundreds of thousands of tons of the best grain to be burned by man's hands to keep grain and bread prices from falling. It must be made impossible to flood mines purposely to keep coal prices up, to leave thousands of good fields untilled so that land owners achieve higher prices, for German factories to deliver cannons, submarines and guns and ammunition to foreign countries. All this can be avoided and will be avoided automatically if values are not set anymore by money . . . but by work. . . ." The waste of the earth's bounty by market manipulation and the waste of man's limited lifetime on earth in war and in mechanical labors were equally abhorrent to Marut. Unlike the majority of Social Democratic leaders of his time, necessity had taken him beyond the narrow sights of patriotism and expediency to see in war the destruction of man and in drudgery the destruction of the human spirit. These, later, become primary concerns of B. Traven. "Even in heaven I should feel sick if I just had to sit around and eat and eat," Traven writes in *The Death Ship*. "I should feel unhappy in a communist state where the community takes all the risks I want to take myself." The need for work that will make men feel useful and enrich their lives is Traven's theme whether he expresses it by describing a meaningless search for gold in *The Treasure of the Sierra Madre* or in novels about the brutalities inflicted upon Indian laborers in the mahogany jungles of Mexico.

12

His concern with these problems can be traced back to that first issue of *Der Ziegelbrenner* when, reaching beyond the censor's ken, he also obliquely expressed his own thoughts in his translations of three poems by Shelley: "Ozymandias," that king of kings, seen in the new light of the Kaiser's Germany, the colossal remaining wreck of power; "Tomorrow," with its irony about hope for the future; "Time," the unfathomable sea, "brackish with the salt of human tears."

### TIME*

Unfathomable Sea! whose waves are years,
Ocean of Time, whose waters of deep woe
Are brackish with the salt of human tears!
Thou shoreless flood, which in thy ebb and flow
Claspest the limits of mortality,
And sick of prey, yet howling on for more
Vomitest thy wrecks on its inhospitable shore;
Treacherous in calm, and terrible in storm,
   Who shall put forth on thee,
   Unfathomable Sea?

Later, Marut also featured Shelley's prose "Declaration of Rights," written in Dublin in 1812, and translated as *Die Menschenrechte.*

---

* ZEIT
    Unergründliches Meer, dessen Wellen Jahre sind!/Weltmeer der Zeit, dessen Gewässer tiefen Whe's/Salzig sind von dem Salze menschlicher Tränen!/Du uferloses Gewoge, das Du in Deiner Ebbe und in Deiner Flut/Umarmst die Grenzen der Sterblichkeit/Und überdrüssig des Raubes, dennoch heulend um mehr/Deine Wracks erbrichst auf ihrem ungastlichen Gestade!/Verräterisch in der Ruhe und schreckenverbreitend im Sturm/Wer soll wohl hinausfahren auf Dir?/Unergründliches Meer?

# 3 Traven's Mysterious Relationship to the Kaiser

A most incongruous note appears on the "theater page" of *Der Ziegelbrenner* under the headline "Thrift, Horatio, Thrift!" There is a sweeping attack on *The King's Players* by a Viennese playwright, Hans Müller. Marut dismisses the play as a "lot of junk." He condemns the playwright for having written a newspaper article about his audience with Kaiser Wilhelm II who "spoke a few kind words for the play." He accuses Müller of "incredible and mean tactlessness, lack of taste and disgusting indiscretion against the German emperor who was so innocently trusting as to have a conversation with Hans Müller. . . ." Marut declared that Müller showed no understanding of "the politeness and good humor that come out of the warm heart of an emperor." The emperor's "good taste in theater questions is generally known," Marut pointed out, but His Royal Highness could scarcely criticize a Viennese playwright while he was a guest of the Viennese court.

Since the Kaiser's own verbal indiscretion with the press had shaken world capitals, such delicate consideration is as astonishing to find in the fiery pages of *Der Ziegelbrenner* as would be a lyric poem by Robert Lowell honoring President Johnson's patronage of the arts in the second act of *MacBird*.

The only way this strange passage makes any sense is in light of rumors that the man now known as the novelist B. Traven was the son of the Kaiser. German reporter Gerd Heidemann wrote in *Stern* magazine (May 7, 1967) that Rosa Elena Luján, the novelist's wife, had told him that her husband believed he was Wilhelm's son. Traven's mother, an actress, had told him so when he was already fighting the Kaiser and his system. (Señora Luján later denied that she had revealed this story.) *Stern* published photographs of the Kaiser, Traven, and two of the Kaiser's six children:* the only sur-

---

*Of the six, Crown Prince Wilhelm's photographs show the closest similarity to

viving one, Viktoria Luise, and the late Crown Prince Wilhelm. There is a remarkable resemblance. The Kaiser's oldest legitimate son was born on May 6, 1882, some two months after the February 25, 1882 birth date Ret Marut had given to Dusseldorf police.

Kaiser Wilhelm II, married at the age of 22 on *February 25, 1881,* was the son of Frederick III, a kind-hearted and liberal man, and Princess Victoria, the highly emotional, opinionated daughter of England's Queen. He suffered from the birth injuries of a shortened left arm and impaired hearing in his left ear. Wilhelm II grew up torn between two ideals: the Prussian Junker and the English gentleman. Kaiser Wilhelm said that he got both his stubbornness and his interest in the arts from his British mother. The Kaiser was also fascinated by archeology, and he published articles on naval strategy under a pseudonym. An objective and perceptive biography by Michael Balfour shows him as a shy and uneasy man, boisterous, too talkative and bolstered by his conviction of the divine right of the Hohenzollern kings; a man with an acute lack of self-confidence behind his favorite pose of iron resolve. Taut and restless, he escaped into a world reshaped unrealistically to his own vision. He was in fact always acting a part. In a large repertoire, three roles were his particular favorites, those of Frederick the Great, of the English milord and Bismarck. Although he was intensely interested in the theater, music and art, "his interference in matters of taste made him highly unpopular in artistic circles." Balfour concludes: "When all the criticisms have been passed, one has the feeling that this was only half the man and that there was another half and one as alive to his own deficiencies as any of the critics."

Was he the father of that equally divided man, B. Traven? Traven himself may not have known the truth. But the fact remains that someone in Germany, someone of considerable importance, protected—and perhaps subsidized—an "alien" radical anti-war editor in the midst of World War I.

---

Traven. His son, Prince Wilhelm of Prussia, died of battle wounds on May 26, 1940, in France while serving with the Nazi armies. On June 17, 1940, the day France fell, the Kaiser, in exile in Doorn in occupied Holland, sent a telegram of congratulations to Hitler whom he had long scorned. "Under the deeply moving impression of the capitulation of France, I congratulate you and the whole German Wehrmacht on the mighty victory granted by God, in the words of the Emperor Wilhelm the Great in 1870: 'What a turn of events brought about by divine dispensation.' " The Kaiser's fourth son, Prince August Wilhelm, was a fanatical Nazi and leader in the SS. As the storm gathered and broke on Europe, Ret Marut, now B. Traven, was far away in the loneliness and safety of Mexico.

There may have been a germ of truth in each of the conflicting stories Marut/Traven gave about his parentage. If his mother was from Great Britain, Marut could have claimed British nationality, and if she had traveled to the United States, where she was unknown, to have her child, he could have claimed American citizenship. One wonders if Marut just felt a sense of identity with Herman Bang's Joán, Prince of "No-country," or if Marut's story had inspired Bang. It is not inconceivable that they had met. Bang, a roving journalist, known as the Danish Oscar Wilde, worked in Berlin and Vienna and associated mainly with artists and performers of all kinds. His *Denied a Country* was first published in 1906, a time when Marut was listed as a supporting actor on German theater programs.

Marut's obsession with illegitimacy and his interest in the theater are both demonstrated in the theater notes of *Der Ziegelbrenner*'s first issue. He praised Strindberg's *Crown Bride,* a laconic play on the folk tale motif of an unmarried mother who murders her child, as a "mighty drama," superior in some ways to Goethe's *Faust.*

## 4 Ret Marut Warns the Germans Against Racial Superiority, but Reflects Confusion Himself

*Der Ziegelbrenner,* in November 1918, was strongly anti-nationalistic; Marut showed the foresight to dissect the racist theories of Houston Stewart Chamberlain, "one of the strangest Englishmen who ever lived." Few Americans know anything about Chamberlain or that he played a significant part in stimulating German racism.

Many Nazis considered Chamberlain the spiritual founder of the Third Reich. Although he was the son of an English admiral and nephew of a British field marshal, Chamberlain was greatly impressed first by his Prussian tutor and then by Richard Wagner who became his father-in-law. In Germany, Chamberlain joined the Gobineau Society, named in honor of a French count who wrote a four-volume essay, *The Inequality of Human Races,* expounding race as the key to history and civilization. In turn, Chamberlain wrote *Foundations of the 19th Century* in 1898, propagating the view that the way to salvation lies in the Teutonic race. The book profoundly influenced both Kaiser Wilhelm II and Adolf Hitler. Years later, Chamberlain, ill and disillusioned by Germany's defeat in the First World War, was swept off his feet by Hitler who visited him in Bayreuth in 1923. "You have mighty things to do," he wrote to Hitler the next day. "With one stroke, you have transformed the state of my soul."

Back in 1918, Marut had already recognized the path to destruction in Chamberlain's philosophy. He bluntly called him a "liar" and wrote that "a German who would have conducted himself in England as this Englishman has in Germany would have been spit upon in Germany. . . .A man who has had the great fortune to write about Goethe uses his editorial ability to throw the people of Germany into an abyss of destruction. If he is so enchanted with Germany, why didn't he go to the trenches? All the men have gone who haven't talked this much about Germany's destiny. If I were an enemy foreigner and I had a plan to make the German people ready for destruction . . . I would have done it exactly as Houston Stewart

**17**

Chamberlain has done here in Germany. It was he who managed to give the Germans the ridiculous idea that Germany was called upon to take world dominion away from England and practice it themselves. It was he who injected the German people with the bacillus of the superiority complex to throw it into the deepest decay that can happen to a people. . . . [He is] responsible for the blood of German sons. . . . Whatever the German people have done in destroying their own people seems blood-white compared to the murderous writings of this man. . . ."

"Fortunately," wrote Marut, "the German people possess neither the brutality nor the rawness, the disrespect or egotistical greed or thoughtless bloodthirstiness nor the feeling of despising people . . . necessary to carry out world domination successfully." Although history would force him to see the bitter error of those words, he *did* know in 1917, with uncanny prescience, that Germany had to be protected "from ever achieving the ability to become a world power." He believed that a poem by Goethe did more honor to the country than the ability to compete successfully on world markets.

Marut himself, attacked by both Jews and anti-Semites, asserted that he was neither a Jew nor an anti-Semite. "If I said that I'm terribly proud of being 100 per cent Teutonic then I would be lying. I'm not proud of it. I can't help it. I had just as little to do with my parentage as with my nationality, be it German, Persian or Chinese."

When the anti-Semitic poet Dietrich Eckart, who later became a friend of Hitler's, implied that Marut was a Jew, the editor answered, ". . . I stand in my own world . . . I find no relationship to Eckart and his friends nor to the Jews. I can't stand a person who proclaims his Jewishness just as I can't stand a person who underlines his anti-Semitism. To me only the person counts *but even with him I only want contact under specific conditions* [my italics]. The German has developed into a person who tries to satisfy his desires for world power so he can have a better export business, and a Jew satisfies himself with the good business he did before the war. Therefore, the anti-Semitic German has really become the Jew, the Jew who loses sleep over the beautiful business with the English grocers, and the Jew has acquired the German view that loss of spiritual cultural good is sadder than the action of railroad shares. . . ."

For all of his independent radicalism, however, there are signs that Marut was not immune to the virus of anti-Semitism. He wrote that "the people who came closest to me in friendship were mostly Jews, but sadly I have to admit—and I stress the word sadly—I haven't found any decent people among them. At one certain point

**18**

where it counts, hard tact or greatness, they suddenly failed always and all of them, maybe this was because I expected too much of people . . . Two other people have proven that these expectations could be fulfilled. These however were Germans and aristocrats by birth and name. But I don't want to lower myself and say that just because of my own painful experience among Jews there are no decent people. If I didn't find them that's only my own fault, so why should I become an anti-Semite?''

He continued, his tone changing as it often does into angry desperation about the follies of the human race: ''Whether Jew or German, Czech or Slovak, French or Japanese, Italian or American, you're all the same pack and the same mob. The Czech will suppress the German just the same as it seemed unbearable to him to be suppressed and specifically you, Jew, are not any better because as long as you say 'I'm a Jew and proud to be one' . . . you're just as bad as an anti-Semite and the only reason you're not anti-Aryan is because you're now in the minority. . . . You cry 'Zion' and I cry back 'earth.' That already proves to me that you belong to the same worms as the others. The name doesn't do anything, Jew, so stay away from me. I'm looking for people.''

Marut constantly tried to point out the ironies and contradictions in the nationalist Christian's profession of faith, as well as the dichotomies within Judaism. But this shrillness* in the work of a man who understood the evil of anti-Semitism is difficult to understand today. However, at that time, anti-Semitism had infected all of Europe, just as the poison of segregation in America also eats into the souls of white men who pride themselves on their belief in equality.

Significantly, Recknagel's book, *B. Traven, Materials for a Biography,* omits almost every reference to Jews. The passage quoted above is reduced to a statement that Marut had a small circle of friends including Jews and two people who were German aristocrats. If I were writing in Germany today, I think I would make the same deletions. But I believe there are still lessons for Americans to learn from Germany's past, as painful as they may be. It is not easy for either Germans or Jews to look back dispassionately at that other

---

* This tone disappears when Marut leaves Germany and its racial obsessions and begins writing as Traven. I would like to believe that the rejection of Marut he expressed in one conversation with me signifies a rejection of this type of writing. He dismissed Marut as a ''political charlatan;'' however, he did not specifically deny that he had been Marut. At the time I interviewed him, when he was still clinging to his identity as ''Hal Croves,'' I had not yet read translations of *Der Ziegelbrenner.* I later raised questions about anti-Semitism and the Bavarian period in a letter to him—but he did not reply.

comparatively safe world in which German Jews prided themselves on their assimilation and their superiority to Eastern European Jews, at a time when Jewish radicals and Jewish businessmen were mortal enemies. When that world went up in smoke, so too did all class and political quarrels.

Although Marut emphasized that he wanted to be without political friends, his closest political affinity was to the Jewish radicals on Bavaria's postwar scene. As a man hostile to all nationalism and clerical hypocrisy, he must have felt free to call the shots as honestly as he saw them, no matter how brutal they might sound to us, 40 years later. But I also believe that Marut's own clouded origin lies at the heart of this matter as with so many aspects of his work. If a man cannot *prove* his birth or nationality, he knows how little they really mean, but at the same time, he must feel forced to find refuge in despising those who take pride in their own people, their own families and country. "Destroy all documents!" cries the schoolteacher in Traven's *General from the Jungle.*

I thought of Traven when I read in *The Fire Next Time,* by James Baldwin: ". . . the father-son relationship is one of the most crucial and dangerous on earth, and to pretend that it can be otherwise really amounts to an exceedingly dangerous heresy . . . It is to be doubted that any of us ever do [get over it] and I think we do ourselves a disservice when we pretend that we have, and substitute the lie of our indifference for the truth of our pain. The truth of our pain is all we have, it is the key to who we are."

If that is the key to the complex mystery of B. Traven, it is, in another sense, also the key to the first tragedy of so many German Jews who were unable to say, with Marut's friend, Gustav Landauer, "My Germanism and my Jewishness do each other no harm but much good ... I accept my complexity and hope to be a unity of even greater complexities than I am aware of."

**Background to Revolution:
the Split Within the German Jews**

Marut's preoccupation with Christianity and Judaism can be better understood in the light of the terrible division among German Jews, a split illustrated in the lives of the Jewish radicals he knew during the Bavarian Revolution: Eisner, Landauer, Ernst Toller, Eric Mühsam and Eugen Leviné. With the exception of Landauer, they all rejected their Jewish heritage.

In his eloquent autobiography, *I Was a German,* Toller told about his 13 months in the trenches before he was released, an invalid and a disillusioned man: ". . . [I was] filled with a passionate desire to prove at the risk of my life that I was a German, nothing but a German. From the front I wrote to the court to erase my name from the Jewish rolls. Was all that in vain? . . . I wanted to repudiate my mother; I am ashamed of myself. That a child was compelled to resort to such lies, what a horrible indictment against all who drove him to it . . . Must I succumb to the madness of my persecutors and accept Jewish instead of German arrogance? Arrogance and love are not synonymous, and if anyone asked me where I belonged, my answer would be: a Jewish mother brought me into this world, Germany has nourished me, Europe has educated me, my home is this earth, and the world my fatherland."

German Jews achieved their full emancipation from the ghetto only after 1871. They were given their first civil liberties by the French under Napoleon, but even that was no gift: the Jews of Frankfurt had to pay 440,000 gulden for the right to civil equality. After Napoleon's defeat the Germans reimposed degrading distinctions on these "friends of the French." "Even Goethe, the choicest spirit of the new Germany was the leader in a movement to reimpose humiliating distinctions about the Jews of Saxe-Weimar," a Jewish historian records. There were Jews who opted for baptism and assimilation: some lived with that choice easily and others were torn by it. A few became violently anti-Semitic. Others chose to work for all of

21

humanity through socialism or anarchism. For those who know Traven's novels, it is unexpected to come upon his involvement with five Jewish radicals whom history has forgotten in the "unknown revolution" in Bavaria.

Kurt Eisner, the son of a Jewish munitions manufacturer, had fought against militarism since 1907 within the Social Democratic Party. He was a witty theater critic and ironic writer, but his parody of a supposedly fictitious "Kaiser" in *Kritik* brought him nine months in jail in 1897. And the anti-militarist stance he shared with Karl Liebknecht proved not very influential among the Social Democrats. The party's executive board met on August 3, 1914, to decide how its 110 members in the Reichstag should vote the next day on appropriations for conducting a war in which Germany would be allied with Austria-Hungary against Serbia and Russia. Twenty Social Democratic leaders were for an affirmative vote on war credits, 14 against—but they decided to voice unanimous support for the majority decision. "Considering what later proved to have been at stake—the whole future of 20th century socialism," historian J. P. Nettl commented, "the discussion was flat and brief."*

Even Eisner wrote in those first days of August 1914, "Now Czarism has attacked Germany, we have no choice, there is no looking back." Not too long afterward, he did look back and became convinced that the Russian armies had not been fully mobilized until the last day of July—four days later than he had been led to believe, and well after Germany's decision to join the conflict became irrevocable. By Easter 1917, he had had enough of the majority Socialist viewpoint and helped found the Independent Social Democratic Party to work for peace without annexation. As the war came to an end, both Socialist factions cooperated uneasily in Bavaria, designating Eisner as first chairman of the Council of

---

* Some German Socialists honestly believed that, as the advance guard of the European working class, it was their responsibility to fight the Czar, the most reactionary force in Europe, but the minority, with a deeper vision, understood the imperialist forces at work on all sides. This basic split on the nature of the war widened with the success of the Bolshevik Revolution. It grew to murderous proportions following World War I when the majority Social Democrats, in power and terrified at the possibility of a thorough revolution, squashed their fellow Socialists with all the arms at their command. This terrible fratricidal war strengthened the conservative forces until Hitler triumphed over them all. Despite years of common persecution, despite all the dead and buried, that early split is still tragically reflected in the Socialist Unity Party of East Germany.

Workers. In the absolute chaos of those days, a crowd marched to the Landtag building and Eisner bloodlessly proclaimed the end of the Wittelsbach dynasty and the founding of the Bavarian Republic. He became its provisional prime minister.

His leadership came under fire from all sides. The press attacked the little man from Berlin as a foreigner and a Jew and declared that he was unfit to lead Bavarian Catholics. A delegation of bourgeois Jews asked him to resign as prime minister in order not to bring harm upon the Jewish community. Later conservative Jewish leaders ran conspicuous ads condemning the Jewish revolutionaries—an attack that Ret Marut commented on with great bitterness. Although Eisner was in favor of a government developed through the new Soldiers' and Workers' Councils, he went along with majority Socialist demands for the election of a National Assembly, elections which Marut attacked as premature and dangerous. When they were held on January 12, 1919, Eisner suffered a disastrous defeat. Shortly afterward, he traveled to Switzerland to acknowledge publicly Germany's war guilt at a meeting of the Second International, and to Germans he became "more than ever the most cursed man in Europe." The Nazis later used Eisner's war guilt documents to "prove the betrayal of Germany by the Jews," and Hitler wrote in *Mein Kampf* that "Eisner's death only hastened the development and finally led to the dictatorship of the councils, or, better expressed, to a passing role of the Jews, as had been the original aim of the instigation of the whole revolution."

When Eisner was murdered, Marut ironically noted that the Jewish revolutionary was called a "foreign despot" but that the Jewish-Italian assassin, Count Arco-Valley, was "called a part of Bavaria. In his honor, great anti-Semitic demonstrations are held, he is given all honors and the public whore [the press] knows long in advance that his sentence will be commuted, probably to life imprisonment." *Der Ziegelbrenner's* prediction was accurate. Count Arco was released from jail on April 17, 1924. In the riotous confusion that followed Eisner's death, a Soviet Republic, opposed by the Communists, was established. There is some evidence that a few Social Democrats provoked the action, aware that a Soviet Republic was doomed to failure. Landauer, Toller, Mühsam and Marut played a part in this first Red Republic.

Although Landauer, an anarcho-syndicalist, saw into the coercive nature of any state, he viewed revolution as a regenerating force and came to its support. A tall, thin, "Christ-like" figure, with a mild manner and soft voice, he was an authority on Shakespeare and had translated Kropotkin and Walt Whitman into German. He saw Whitman as the embodiment of the conservative and the revolutionary spirit, uniting individualism and socialism. Landauer advocated passive resistance and nonviolence, looking for cooperative enterprises on the land as the way of social change.

Landauer, a close friend of Martin Buber's, could see both the sadness and humor of his revolutionary role (similar qualities illuminate the work of his grandson, Mike Nichols, the actor and director). On a postcard bearing his own picture, he wrote to a friend: "I am now the commissar for propaganda, science, art and a few other things. If I am allowed a few weeks time I hope to accomplish something; but there is a bare possibility that it will only be a couple of days and then it will have been but a dream." During this period, Marut was Landauer's associate and developed a program for socialization of the press and indemnification of the owners.

That first Soviet government lasted six days. The majority Social Democrats who had won the January elections tried to regain power in a Palm Sunday *putsch* under the new Prime Minister Johannes Hoffmann, but failed. A governing Factory and Soldiers Council of Munich was formed and named Eugen Leviné as head. Leviné, a Communist who was a native of Russia had participated in the 1905 Russian Revolution, later became a German citizen and served in the German Army. Defying orders from the Communist Party in Berlin, he headed the second Soviet government. When it was defeated, he was court-martialed and executed at the age of 36.

Landauer, 56, was murdered on May 2. He was dragged and kicked into a court yard by White officers, beaten with truncheons, shot and trampled upon. Before he died, he told the soldiers, "I have not betrayed you. You don't know yourselves how terribly you have been betrayed."

His tragic death was recorded by Toller, who was arrested and sentenced to five years' imprisonment for his role as a leader of the first Soviet government and commander of the Red Army in Dachau. Toller was preparing to negotiate a surrender in Munich when he realized that White troops from Berlin had encircled the city, but after they executed some Red stretcher bearers, there were cries for revenge. Landauer and Toller tried to prevent further senseless slaughter, but the commander-in-chief of the Red Army ordered the shooting of nine dangerous political prisoners, conspirators of the right-wing Thule Society who had themselves planned an armed overthrow of the Red Republic. These "hostage murders" were the excuse for the massacre by White troops that followed.

24

Toller, who later became famous for his plays, committed suicide in New York in 1939 at the age of 45, in despair over the fall of Madrid and the imminence of a new world war.

A violent death was also the fate of Mühsam. Often a figure of fun in life, he died with dignity. He had been sentenced in 1919 to 15 years in jail, but was released in 1924 as part of an amnesty for political prisoners which also freed Hitler who had served only eight and a half months of the five-year term for his 1923 beer hall *putsch* in Munich. Mühsam was arrested by the Nazis the day after the Reichstag fire—February 27, 1933—and sent to the concentration camp at Oranienburg. Once described as "anarchistically overstrained," Mühsam, at a worn 56, reacted characteristically when the Nazis aimed their guns and ordered him to sing the Horst Wessel song. Although he was an anarchist and student of Tolstoy, he defiantly sang "The Internationale." The Nazis fired above his head; Mühsam collapsed in a faint. The next day, July 10, 1934, he was found murdered in what the Nazis tried to disguise as suicide.

**Marut, Whose Theological Studies Soured, Defies Death and the Church**

It seems a miracle that Ret Marut managed to escape the fate of his five comrades. He had written much that would lead the authorities to desire him dead. During World War I, he was forced to submit copy for *Der Ziegelbrenner* to the censors, but even so, he found ways to continue to express his opposition. Mocking the slogan of a "lively, happy war," he took aim at those who called war a "liberating blessing" and "an injection of blood and life into sleeping peoples." He could only suggest the role of the press in deliberately printing a premature story about German war mobilization that made it impossible to hold back the momentum of the war machine. He mourned "this terrible time of silence" and repeatedly asked "why the representative of God does not damn into eternity all those who make wars." He continued to drive home this basic question in nearly every novel he wrote as B. Traven.

Marut attacked the sentimentality that surrounds death in war and in life, devoting one issue in March 1918 to a long and forceful poem which he wrote, but which he disguised under the title "The Death Songs of Hyotamore von Kyrena." To outsmart the censors, Marut said they were East Indian songs at least 1000 years old. But, in fact, they expressed Marut's reaction to the war and the meaningless rituals superimposed on the stark fact of death. In later years, as B. Traven, he came to appreciate the joyful death ceremonials of the Mexican Indians which lacked the hypocrisy of European traditions.

After Marut attended funeral services for the dramatist Frank Wedekind, he wrote: "This disgusting funeral made me drive home quickly because now I know for sure that nobody will ever know when I breathe my last breath. The moment I feel my end coming, I'll immediately hide in the thickest shrubbery where no one can follow me and where I will in devotion and reverence await eternity and die without a sound, and go still and silently into the big oneness from whence I have come and I will be thankful to the Gods when the vultures and *rejected* [my italics] dogs will have eaten their fill of my body so that not even a pale bone will be left." (A "hideous" dog turns up later as the only true friend of the king in Marut's fantasy *Khundar,* and a rejected dog is the subject of one of Traven's most moving stories, "Friendship." Fittingly, a mangy dog put in an appearance at the final rites for Traven in Chiapas.)

Marut's "Totengesange" (Death Songs), like B. Traven's "The Cotton Picker's Song," have some of the brutal power of Brecht, although a great deal is inevitably lost in translation. "Why do you weep?" he demands in the "Death Songs": "Because it costs nothing, because it looks good, because it is customary . . . you are hypocrites in any case . . . the richest among you is the dead for he has no more than he needs: peace. See how miserable and petty you are: you adorn the dead with flowers and twigs. Put costly clothes on them, decorate them with gold and precious stones, give them expensive coffins made of fragrant wood or silver, erect solid mausoleums although they are not cold or hungry and the rain does not make them wet. But those who are really hungry and cold and freeze before the storm sweeping across the sea, you let die in misery without caring . . ."*

Even contemplating an after life, Marut doesn't lose his dim view of his fellow man: "The thought that I would have to meet again somewhere all the rabble that I have met quite unnecessarily here on earth would alone induce me not to die."

A fascinating 96-page issue of *Del Ziegelbrenner,* dated January 15, 1919, revealed exactly how wartime censorship had operated. There is also an intriguing aside which refers to a man who was taking responsibility for everything Marut wrote "without batting an eye" and to that man's day-to-day fear that he would end up before a firing squad.

All the disgust that had boiled within Marut during the war now erupted. From ancient times, he pointed out, the highest praise in German countries was to be considered "true and honest," but "in that country where truth is appreciated above all, no one has been so persecuted and harmed as the one who wanted and had to tell the truth because he did not want to suffocate with it." England and

---

*"The billions we spend on our dead would serve mankind better if they were spent on more hospitals, on prepaid doctors' fees, and on more research on disease. It would be more humane and surely more civilized if instead of wasting billions upon the dead, we spent that money on the living to keep them sane and healthy and so have them longer with us. Just on the flowers that are thrown to the dead, who cannot see or smell them, we could save enough money to take care of ten thousand babies every year and make their mothers happy."—*The Bridge in the Jungle* by B. Traven

France permitted merciless criticism against the conduct of the war, he wrote, but it was forbidden in the Reich, particularly against Field Marshal von Hindenburg and General Ludendorff, "two idols we had been told to adore."

Scorning circumlocutions like "credibility gap," Marut acidly declared: "The old Germany has not been destroyed by the over-powering might of its political enemies, not by the victory of other countries, not by the tyranny of militarism and not by its lack of food; it has died of its own lies. These lies ... have smothered Germany and strangled it. A state which feels that it has to use such lies towards its own people in order to save its existence is ripe for destruction. ... With a great lie, the murder of all people began. This war has never been a defensive war; it was an offensive war and Germany prepared for it since the beginning of the '90s."

He cited the details of a story he had previously only hinted at and charged that the *Berliner Lokalanzeiger* had published an extra edition on mobilization 24 hours before a real mobilization order was issued. This story was deliberately planted in a semi-official news-paper, he declared, by those who wanted to see the failure of negotia-tions then underway to prevent war, and to maneuver the German government into a position from which it could not withdraw.

"If I say that the greatest rascal and liar during the war was a journalist," Marut wrote, "I do not forget to add: right after him comes the clergyman. For the representative of Christ on earth there should not be a government—Christ did not know any state, he only knew humanity, he only knew brothers, only children of God. ... But God's representatives did indeed make a difference between God's children in England, in France, in Russia and in Germany. Christ's dogma is not a national òne, it is not even international, it is expressly anti-national. Nowhere does Christ say war is permissible, He does not even mention a defensive war. ... But He did say 'Put away your sword where it belongs; because he who takes up the sword shall perish by the sword.' ... How else could He have said, 'Blessed be the meek for they shall inherit the earth'?"

Marut's pointed, satirical phrase "representative of Christ" for priests and the Pope predated its use by that other iconoclastic German writer, Rolf Hochhuth, author of *The Deputy* (Der Stell-vertreter) who condemned the silence of Pope Pius XII in the face of Nazi persecution of the Jews. *Stellvertreter,* which can be trans-lated as "representative" or "deputy," is not a commonly used synonym for a priest or the Pope in Germany.

In a rare reference to his own life in *Der Ziegelbrenner,* Marut mentioned that he left his theological studies too soon to learn the answer to his question: how could one pray on the pulpit for the victory of the German Army without having Christ descend to scourge "these damned victory-preachers out of His temple?" In fact, as he wrote in *Der Ziegelbrenner,* he was thrown out of the seminary, for asking "indecent questions."\*

"Why," Marut wondered later, "do I occupy myself so much with Christ and his word when the teachings of Buddha are so much closer to me? Because we call ourselves Christians and of the spirit of Christ, we don't have a trace."

When the war ended, Marut wrote that the Germans would only be able to gain the confidence of other countries if "we hold judgment over ourselves with absolute honesty and merciless frankness." He even took on his share of war guilt: instead of working for peace while there was still time, he confessed that he had spent his evenings in dance halls!

He soon learned that there would be as little toleration for "merciless frankness" under the new "People's Government" in Berlin as there had been under the Kaiser's regime. "I got a People's Government," he wrote. "I got it by common law. I did not even notice it, because we only had the *right* to speak of a People's Government. We got no other rights. It has always been the same damned condition, that in Germany one always talked about the

---

\*At the University of Baden, Recknagle reported, there is a notation from 1903 about the expulsion of an American theology student named Charles Trefny of "St. Louis, Miss." who said he had studied at St. Xavier University in Cincinnati, Ohio, but the American school has no record of such attendance. A Joseph Trefney, 68 years old, who lived in St. Louis, told me that his father's parents emigrated from Bohemia, and that his father's uncle was a Catholic priest in St. Louis, Father Trefney. (However, the St. Louis Archdiocese has no record of a Father Trefney.) In Traven's *The Death Ship,* the narrator, an American sailor named Gales, tells about his hard life as a boy of seven in Chicago. Gales worked all day long as a milkman's assistant and newsboy until he "fell like a stone on the bare floor of a room on Lincoln Avenue, in which I was allowed to sleep free of charge for washing dishes at night for a German clergyman who had fled from his country on account of having, like a true gentleman, sworn falsely to save the reputation, if any, of a married jane." Traven denies that he was "Charles Trefny," but it is difficult to imagine that there were *two* theology students with shadowy American backgrounds expelled from German universities in the same period, unless he was drawing, both as Marut and Traven, on the experiences of an acquaintance. It is much more plausible to assume that Marut himself had an extensive theological education after reading his repeated references to the Bible in *Der Ziegelbrenner.*

duties but never of the rights ... particularly in the most lying of all times of history ... Social Democracy has gone along the path which unfortunately has been trodden by every party in Germany so far which originally had revolutionary aims. This imperialistic Social Democracy would never have produced a revolution; it had long been gelded, long been rotten to the core and impotent.''

# 7

## The Individualistic, Anarchistic Philosophy of the Novelist Begins to Develop

Marut's emphasis on the worth of the single individual echoes the philosophy of the German individualistic anarchist Max Stirner. One of the few ads carried by *Der Ziegelbrenner* was for Stirner's work.

In his book *The Ego and Its Own,* Stirner rejected all political and moral ties of the individual and attacked generalized concepts such as right, virtue and duty. He saw the ego not as an anti-moral force but as a philosophy for liberated individualists. Although an egoist could join a party, Stirner said, "he cannot let himself be embraced and taken up *by* the party."

Marut spoke in this vein in the speech *Der Ziegelbrenner* printed on January 30, 1919, under the title "The World Revolution is Starting." "Hello, people!" he hails his audience. "Hello, men and women of the revolution! Hello! Greetings to you, brothers of the coming world republic! Greetings to you, people of the Holy World Citizenship under way! Hello, human beings—Hello! I am neither a member of the Social Democratic Party, nor am I an Independent Socialist. I am neither a member of the Spartacus Group nor am I a Bolshevik. I do not belong to any party, to any political organization, whatever kind it be; this is because neither parties nor programs, neither proclamations nor resolutions taken in meetings can save me from the world's disaster. I cannot belong to any party, because I see in membership in any party a restriction of my personal freedom, because the obligation to follow a party program takes away from me all possibility of developing into that which I consider the highest and noblest goal on earth: *to be a human being!* I do not want to be anything but a human being, just a man. And since 'man' is most important to me, I must remain indifferent to everything else; everything which does not lead me to this goal must be negligible. But such indifference must stop for me when danger lies on my path. And only *for myself* do I raise my voice. This is *My Own* cause, not yours. I am still indifferent to your cause and shall always

**31**

remain so. *THE NOBLEST, PUREST AND MOST SIGNIFICANT HUMAN LOVE IS THAT TO ONESELF!* I want to be free! I myself want to be able to be glad! I am the one who wants to enjoy all the beautiful things on earth. I am the one who wants to be happy. But my freedom is secure only if all other people around me are free. I can be happy *only* if all other people around me are happy, all those I see and meet look out into the world with happy eyes. And ONLY then can I enjoy eating my fill, if I feel sure that other people too are able to sate their hunger, just as I am. And therefore it is my own well-being, only my own self, for which I oppose all danger threatening my freedom and my happiness."

Marut revealed in *Der Ziegelbrenner* that he had warned Social Democrats as far back as 1905 that once the Social Democratic Party gained power, it would become "more brutal" than what they had already experienced under Bismarck. "I felt that Social Democracy was creating a form of popery worse than that of the Catholic Church ... and that is exactly what happened ... And we have to keep our eyes open, because the Communist Party to the left has already found its very strong successor and it could be that once arrived in power, the followers of the successor party could be persecuted by it, just as the Communists are persecuted today by the Social Democrats. To keep the political concept intact, I am so far left that my breath does not even touch that successor."

It is another subject that Traven was to pursue in his novels. "I do not want to judge," he wrote in *The Death Ship*. "Each age and each country tortures its Christians. That which was tortured yesterday is the powerful church today and a religion in decay tomorrow. The deplorable thing, the most deplorable thing, is that the people who were tortured yesterday, torture today. The Communists in Russia are no less despotic than the fascists in Italy or the textile-mill magnates in America. ...."

# 8

## Marut Is Captured, and He Escapes

Traven joined with others for what appears to be the first and last time in his life when, as Marut, he became a member of the "Preparatory Committee to Establish a Revolutionary Tribunal" and a member of the Propaganda Committee during the first Soviet Republic, in charge of censorship of the bourgeois newspapers in Munich.

His role as a revolutionary official ended with the May Day massacre. Marut vividly described his escape from almost certain death in the December 1919 issue.

For the first time, the name of the editor is not listed and the masthead simply states: "To the subscribers he is known." The issue is "put out by an editor in flight and published by a publishing company in flight." Marut reports that his "most faithful companion" (Irene Mermet who had the title of publisher*) "without whose indefatigable activity I would be almost helpless" is being sought for treason and "is fleeing someplace to a decent foreign country that does not claim to be the freest state in the world."

He then tells what happened to him on May 1, 1919. Marut was waiting in a cafe for some other revolutionary writers when

---

*Professor Recknagel reports that Irene Mermet had been in a school for actors under the name of Irene Aldor in 1915. She later worked with Marut in their own publishing house, J. Mermet, which in 1916 issued a novel *An das Fraulein von S . . .* by a writer called Richard Maurhut. The writer enjoyed his little mysteries even then. As Marut, editor of *Der Ziegelbrenner,* he often published ads for Maurhut's novel, which dealt with a front-line soldier whose "heroism" was actually motivated by a desire for death because of an unhappy love affair. When a West Prussian newspaper expressed its suspicion that the two names belonged to one person, Marut commented: "So what? It wouldn't reflect badly on me and Ret Marut would from this moment on be the writer of one of the most wonderful books that has been written in German during the last ten years." His associate Irene also used other names: Irene Alda and Irene Mennet. There are conflicting versions about her life following their flight from Munich. There is a report that she died.

"the cars of the White Guards began to speed through the streets to free Munich from the Red terror. The White Guards did not take the trouble to make long songs and dances. They shot immediately into the masses of people in their Sunday clothes. Immediately after that seven innocent citizens were rolling in their blood. Two died while still in the street. Some steps from the coffee house lay a well-dressed seriously wounded man. While the machine fire of the White Guards went on in a fury, M with others helped to carry the wounded into the coffee house and M left. ... He had hardly taken 100 steps—the streets were still under fire—when a car sped by loaded with about 60 infantry guns and carbines ... [and] employees and students who had white armbands and handkerchiefs around their arms. When they saw M, the car stopped. Five men with guns around them ... threw themselves on M. M asked what the gentlemen wished. They told him he was a member of the central committee, the destroyer of the press, the most dangerous agitator of the Council Republic, destroyer of the bourgeoisie and therefore he was to go with them. If he did not admit he carried the main blame for the bloodbath about to happen, they would make short shrift of him and shoot him. M was searched by each one of the bloodthirsty comedians for weapons, the editor of *Der Ziegel-brenner* searched for weapons! Of course, it is possible to look for truffles on naked roof tiles if one has nothing else to do."

Marut was thrown into a car filled with guns and faced ten pistols aimed at him. The car sped away to the howling cries of "noble freedom fighters and the saviours of the bourgeoisie." To fulfull their need for acclaim, Marut's captors stopped the car before the house of a general, stood at attention, saluted and cried loudly, "May the general live! Hooray! Hooray!" and showed him their "most dangerous" prisoner. "The general, whose presence and quiet stay in his apartment was a sufficient sign of the Bolshevik terror, called down benevolently," Marut reported. "Highly satisfied, as if each one had been promoted to Prussian noncommissioned officer, the courageous fighters for Munich's freedom sped away with their precious booty."

At the War Ministry, Marut was taken down under heavy guard and searched for weapons again. During cross-examination he was accused of about 20 serious crimes of high treason: inducing soldiers to rebel against officers, insulting the majority Socialist regents and advocating use of force against the legal Hoffmann government. The death sentence was to be declared immediately. "M (sic) decided he had nothing to say to that and could not possibly accept as judges these gentlemen who had taken him, a quiet walker, off the streets by force.

"When unable to get anything out of him, one of the gentlemen yelled 'confess now voluntarily or we will get witnesses and then you're done for.' Soon witnesses came who testified to everything according to their wishes. ... These witnesses also played an important role in the processes of the Bavarian kangaroo courts whose activities shall in the future be a more effective testimonial in history to the bestiality, the brutality, hypocrisy and criminality of the German bourgeoisie and the mendacity of the German Social Democrats than the war and the November lie. ..."

The field court consisted of a snappy lieutenant who took three minutes in each case to decide whether the prisoner was to be shot immediately or to be freed. In case of doubt, the prisoner was shot without an opportunity to call defense witnesses.

A tumult suddenly broke out when one man objected to his rough treatment by the soldiers, and in the disturbance Marut managed to escape. "Two soldiers who might have experienced for a minute a spark of humanity when they saw the treatment given to the most precious thing a man has—his life—were not uninvolved in the escape," Marut revealed. "Here they are thanked for the preservation of a human life. In my estimation, there are about 10,000 misguided Reichswehr officers and soldiers known by the fact that they are people and are not under the command of the German Noske. The German people don't need the Reichswehr and Germany will only have the right to say Goethe is a German when no guns, hand grenades or gas bombs can be found in Germany except perhaps in a museum."

While Marut was in flight, hunted, living in empty apartments, in shacks and in the woods, he wondered whether it might not have been better to surrender. When he considered that "the judges are not judges but cheap hangmen," he concluded that it would have been a meaningless gesture. To complete the full measure of the law's disgrace, he noted that the courts are now called "People's Courts." Later, historians were to record that the Weimar Repubic failed to clean out the judiciary, and the administration of the law became one of the centers of the counterrevolution.

Marut, still hopeful for a real revolution, traveled from one village to another talking to small groups of men about the council form of government.

On January 6, 1920, *Der Ziegelbrenner* reported that Marut had been deprived of his home and his food card and was sought for high treason "because M has a different opinion than the Social Democrats as to what is useful to mankind." Marut and Irene would probably leave the dying city of Munich, the paper indicated, adding, "A city or country that wants to die should be allowed to die in peace. If one can, one should even speed up the process."

# 9    In Flight, Marut Furiously Attacks the German Press

In the midst of all this grief, turmoil and flight, Marut took the time to present his weird and incomprehensible essay, "The Destruction of Our World Systems by the Markurve." The publication was stimulated by newspaper reports that experiments by British scientists had confirmed Einstein's theory of relativity, first announced in 1915. Marut modestly estimated that his own theory was two generations in advance of Einstein's. The editor attacked mathematics as a philosophy which requires belief in straight lines, dots, circles and globes that "do not exist anywhere in the world: they can only be imagined and thought ... just as no one can visualize infinity and God. Therefore math is working with exactly the same means as theology. Mathematics has solely imagined 'one' since there is neither 'one' present nor a 'one' imaginable. M concludes that there is no straight line, only a curve of unalterable steadiness of course. The steadiness lies between infinity and the shortest of all time periods and the curve never rests. ... Everything has the body and form of an egg. ...."

Marut wrote that he had planned to announce his philosophy at a later date but advanced publication when he read about the "great sensation Albert Einstein" in the daily press. The butt of Marut's attack is the Ullstein publishing house, which he had previously condemned, along with Scherl Publishers, for their war books and cheap stories, "which threaten to destroy culture and good taste."

Again, a look into the future helps to explain the vehemence of Marut's repeated attacks on the press.

"The German press, especially the 'great press,' represented by the so-called liberal papers of the great publishers Ullstein and Rudolf Mosse or by the *Frankfurter Zeitung,* definitely lacked any sort of fighting spirit," according to Franz Schoenberner, editor of the now deceased satirical weekly *Simplicissimus.* "Even in the early thirties when the simple instinct of self-preservation, if not a feeling of responsibility, should have dictated an all out offensive against the not yet insuperable forces of Nazism ... [they] clung stubbornly to a purely suicidal conception of democratic freedom which evidently included the right of the Nazis to kill democracy. ... The deeper reason ... was of course that every dictator, whatever his criminal record, could count upon the deep sympathy of all 'vested interests' in the world, as long as he recommended himself as a 'bulwark against the Communist danger.' "

It is dismaying to read the autobiography of Herman Ullstein, one of five brothers in the Ullstein publishing firm which was among the Jewish publishing houses the Nazis forced out of business. The firm was founded by their father, Leopold Ullstein, in 1877. "Of Jewish origin himself," wrote Herman, "he had his sons brought up in the Christian faith because, as he said, the state we were destined to serve was Christian."

When in 1928, he decided "it was the duty of the Ullsteins to combat Hitler," Herman was outvoted because "the House of Ullstein could not afford to have opinions." Herman was eventually forced to leave Germany with only ten marks, but amazingly, he could still record that he felt "hopeful" about the future even after Hitler was appointed chancellor on January 30, 1933. The Nazis had ordered the newspapers to advise their readers to vote for Hitler in the March 5 election; they had ordered stories on crimes committed by Jews and they had abolished political parties. Despite all this, Ullstein wrote: "There were times, as a matter of fact, when Goering, now in charge of the press, was quite tractable and even increased our hopes of a modus vivendi. Alone among the National Socialists, he had a sense of humor. ... This led to fresh hopes that, although the newspapers in the future would have to remain uncritical, they might at least be allowed some independent existence."

To Marut, there was no mystery about why the Ullstein press had suddenly raised "Einstein to a new height in world history." Subscription prices had gone up, there was no news about war, about mass murders in Russia or its "socialization of women" and a counter-balance was needed to offset the effect of some "less savory" stories involving Jews. Marut felt that there were better ways than this to eliminate anti-Semitic pogroms. Anti-Semitism would not abate, he declared, "as long as Jewish money is given freely to put down the Red Republic in Russia where Jewish pogroms can't happen; as long as Jewish money is given away in Germany to prevent by all means recognition of humanity and love of peace. ..." Querulously, he demanded: "If a new great of world history would be a non-Jew for a change and by coincidence one who is tolerated by the whores because they need subscriptions, would the pimps sacrifice the whole front page? But it's all right: the biggest honor really is to be ignored by the press ... Oh, you German-speaking people! A pimp [newspaperman] said: 'We may have lost the war but German science is celebrating its highest triumph'. ... In that phrase ... lies the whole misery of today's life, the whole distress in which humanity is thrown through the press ... It's the misery of the soul and humanity, the destruction of mankind, that is what makes one sad or fills one with furious rebellion. I choose the latter."

# 10 A Rebellion Muted in Lyric Fantasy

A few months later, Marut's "furious rebellion" was muted into an elegiac tone with the publication of his lyric fantasy "Khundar" in *Der Ziegelbrenner*. It was Marut's formal envoi to Germany, written for the Germans "in a time of tears" when "dark forces" again began to judge and rule the land. The poet and singer Khundar reflects Marut's own complex feelings, poignantly split between his rejection by the Germans and his rejection of them. Perhaps he sees himself as their saviour when he watches the mythical King's funeral and asks, "Doesn't he have a son to follow him?" It is in the plaintive, tender key touched once before when Marut wrote about the emperor and the playwright and it again raises the question of whether Marut knew for a certainty that the Kaiser was his father.

As Khundar watched the King's funeral, he heard the muffled echo of the kettledrums. A page carried the King's crown on his pillow and the people said: "He gave the heavy crown away when the people were hungry and he said: 'It's better to save a person than to have gold and valuables.'"

"Then another page came. He carried a scepter on his pillow. It was made of ash, carved by a charcoal burner. And the king had spoken to him: 'You are a person, charcoal burner, and I am a person, good as you are and bad as you are. Why should I carry the sign of a judge in my hands—no person on earth can be judge over another person. How could I do justice to people with power, the executioner's axe and the hangman's noose? If you have a battle about your land, I will measure and balance and give my decision. But those who have an official position in this land are stronger than I am and they don't act this way because they are full of greed.'"

In the procession, no one was as sad as a hideous dog, the King's favorite, who broke loose from his leash and jumped into the funeral pyre . . . "and they left the dog because no one else had acted like the dog and still every one of the people said they had loved the king.''

Khundar stayed at the rear of the procession with sad eyes and drooping, grieving shoulders until he met an old man to whom he exclaimed:

"That is a king's funeral! Oh that is a king's death! But isn't it as though only business men were together who had brought off a deal, punctually and honestly and with net profit? And no one cries. And I am a foreigner here and it touches me. Didn't the king deserve one single friend to cry over him?''

Then the old man said: "A king has always deserved a friend, but has a king ever had a friend? Has a friend ever cried over a king? Maybe the stable man because he gave him a good salary and now he has to collect!''

Then Khundar said: "Not one friend, in life not one friend and yet a king! I also have no friend. I am all alone. . . .''

"Doesn't he have a son to follow him?'' asks Khundar.

"And if he had one, wouldn't the son laugh because his father died and he is the heir? The dog cried because of the man; not the son, not the friend and not the wife,'' replies the old man.

Khunder meets a young woman who is now ruler of the land. She appears to symbolize Germany and she falls in love with Khundar. The old man tells him that she is having a child, "cutting this child herself out of her own heart.''

"Out of her own heart? Out of her own heart?'' said Khundar amazed. "What pain she must suffer!''

"Oh, what pain a person suffers when he realizes he is a person among those who are not people,'' said the old man.

Marut begins to exorcise his own pain as the poetic fantasy proceeds, although, Khundar says that his heart is dead and his soul is empty: "My thoughts are wandering through far worlds, past eternities and I stand in the midst of them. Oh soul, my soul, how you search. Do you search a second soul to be complete in all eternity?''

The man who forever searches for his second soul is also attuned to the soul in lifeless things. Khundar's sensitivity to the life in a piece of iron or the song of a bird as he makes his final journey through the land reappears in a variety of situations in Traven's novels. When Khundar and the Queen pause at a smithy's shop, there is a human quality to the rebellious iron, "red with anger'' because "it wants to stay what it was and didn't want to become what the

**41**

blacksmith forced it to become." The iron is one of many "apparently lifeless things" which "really have souls like humans."

The blacksmith refuses to take the Queen's emerald because he can't eat it or drink it. This foreshadows Traven's emphasis on the soil as the eternal verity of man's life—for the basic sustenance it provides, not for its gold (*The Treasure of the Sierra Madre*) or its oil (*Rosa Blanca*).

When the Queen asks Khundar, "Why do you sing your most beautiful songs and never ask who listens and who carries them further?" Khundar tells her to "ask the blackbird why he sings and why he doesn't care if you listen or not." Traven's Doc Cranwell in *The Night Visitor* is in the blackbird's tradition—he wrote his books in the jungle for the pleasure of writing and then destroyed them. "Fame," says the doc, "is the bunk."

And "Khundar" contains an indication of Traven's attitude to the revelation of his life story: "A big book mounted with silver and locked with a narrow bolt . . . followed the dead king and should be burned with him. In it, he had written down every day of his life, everything he had thought, everything he had done and what he had seen and no person should know what the king had written in his lonely hours. And that book was now carried with him to the grave."

The woman who loves Khundar is eager to hear his words and she asks him to talk to her of "wisdom, truth and love," but he does not reply. "His eyes were turned away from everything that connected him with the earth, deep in thought about the salvation of humanity which is born in the heart and far from the noise of the world."

She finally embraces him and dies and Khundar walks through the city where the people are searching for their Queen. In the sunset, he sees the King's castle collapse and turn "once again to the stone of which it was built, but stones will talk where the hearts of the people bleed. Salvation will come to the people through tears and much pain and much sorrow. Salvation will come through questions and searching and wandering! Therefore, let us go wandering only where there is truth, wisdom, salvation and light.

"And when he had so spoken, he left from there into a far country that same evening."

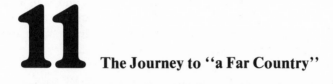

## 11 The Journey to "a Far Country"

On the journey to that far country of Mexico, the man Khundar, the man Marut, disappeared, cutting forever his ties to Europe, and a writer named B. Traven made his appearance on the world's literary scene. There are paradoxes, more mysteries and many adventures in the life that followed.

When Traven wrote, "An unanswered question flutters about you for the rest of your life," I believe he was saying that the mystery of his birth would plague him forever. All else that is unknown in his life is peripheral. In his novel of 1916 *An das Fraulein von S . . .* , the soldier at the front says

> I have only one thought. What do I care about life and
> country? What is the world to me? And what is the war to
> me and the stormy awakening of an entire people to a united,
> mighty will? For I am alone, all alone, so alone and lonely
> as only a human can be who suddenly awakens and, as if
> enlightened, perceives that nobody on earth, not one human
> being, not even his mother, is related to him in his deepest
> existence, that love and faith are nothing more than pure
> egoism.

I wonder: did a lonely child wake up one dark night and invent a friend to comfort him, someone to whom he could tell the deepest secrets of his heart? Ret Marut/Richard Maurhut. Hal Croves/ B. Traven. Was the iconoclastic theological student named Charles Trefny? How does a sensitive, imaginative youth protect himself when he has to bring the nonexistent documents of his life to school, the police and the issuers of passports? What defenses does he develop to maintain his dignity and privacy? What indeed if the young rebel learns—true or false—that he is the son of the man whose system he rebels against? To cover hurt and insecurity, can he only loudly declare that he "does not give a damn" for the opinions of others? Vulnerable, he writes, "I am invulnerable. Because what I do is law, because I do it. I'm the judge regarding my actions. No one else."

In the final analysis, B. Traven is right: all that matters is the truth or the falsity in his work and in his work, as we shall see, he strives to tell the truth. It was not B. Traven who sought out the press, it was the press who searched for him. But it is the people who care about his value as a writer who want to learn more about him as a human being. When *Stern* magazine asked the Kaiser's grandson, Prince Louis Ferdinand, the head of the House of Hohenzollern, about B. Traven, he coldly replied: "I consider the entire matter closed." If Traven was indeed a Hohenzollern, may I suggest it is for *them* to take pride in the relationship, but only for that final truth expressed in "Khundar": "The king is a human being! The human being is king!"

# Part Two: Conversations With B. Traven

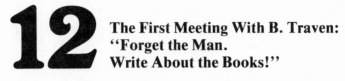

# 12 The First Meeting With B. Traven: "Forget the Man. Write About the Books!"

I had been nervous enough about intruding on a man who had gone to incredible lengths to guard his privacy for 40 years and more, but I felt immediately defeated when I first met B. Traven in the patio of his home off Mexico City's tree-lined boulevard, the Reforma. I realized that he was almost totally deaf, despite a hearing aid. He shook hands unsmilingly and sat down, uneasily clasping his heavily veined hands in his lap. His bright blue eyes looked sad behind thick spectacles, his long white hair still showed a blond tinge, and his bony face, punctuated by a domineering nose, was severe. Although he appeared frail, with a cautious step and a nervously nodding head, his short wiry frame conveyed an impression of the strength and energy that must have served him as a young man.

I made some feeble attempts to offer what I hoped was a reassuring smile, but his eyes refused to meet mine. After grumbling a bit about the lack of a new battery for his hearing aid, he suddenly cried out in English, accented by German: "Forget the man! What does it matter if he is the son of a Hohenzollern prince or anyone else? Write about his works. Write how he is against anything which is forced upon human beings, including communism or Bolshevism. See how, among all Traven's books, there goes one thought like a red thread from the first line of his first book to the last line of his last book. Since he doesn't want to be a reformer or preacher, he lets the reader get the red thread."

The impact of that "one thought" had hit me for the first time many years ago when I saw a book title, succinct and powerful, *The Rebellion of the Hanged*. With deceptive simplicity, the author had laid bare the miserable lives of poor Mexican Indians. I wondered how someone with such an un-Mexican sounding name could have had the insight to dramatize that suffering with so much humor and understanding, leading up to a crescendo of violence and brutality.

But it was not until I decided to visit Mexico in 1964 that I was hooked by the Traven "mystery." Browsing in a bookstore, I found a paperback collection of short stories, *The Man Nobody Knows,* which noted that the author lived in Mexico City. A friend suggested that I could learn more about Traven from Philip Stevenson, a novelist and Hollywood scriptwriter who had written the screenplay for *Rosa Blanca*—the Mexican film made in 1962 but not released at that time. Stevenson predicted that I would not be able to interview Traven, but gave me the name of his "agent," Hal Croves. However, a check at the library disclosed that in the late '40s a Mexican reporter and novelist, Luis Spota, had tracked down Traven as the man Croves who had been an advisor to John Huston during the filming of *The Treasure of the Sierra Madre.* Croves' card gave Acapulco as his address and it was known that he traveled on an American passport.

Spota had checked Mexican immigration records and discovered on Form 14 for Registry of Foreigners, dated July 12, 1930, the name of Berick Traven Torsvan, born in Chicago on May 3, 1890, the son of Scandinavian parents. He went to Acapulco, where he found his man, known to the neighbors as El Gringo, living in quarters at the rear of a beer and refreshment stand, Torsvan/ Croves had lived there since 1933, and spent much of his time tending the mango and cashew trees in his orchard. Spota bribed a servant to intercept Torsvan's mail. When a letter arrived with a royalty payment in Swiss francs for B. Traven, Spota confronted him with it. Croves protested that Traven was his cousin, had left Mexico and was a patient in a sanitarium in Davos, Switzerland, and that he, Torsvan, had adopted the name years before. He indicated that he was merely one of the collaborators on whom the real Traven was dependent, and therefore he received some payments in Traven's name. In a farewell gesture, he served Spota a dinner of roast goose and told him a Travenesque story about a man who had gone hunting for wild goose and had found a ghost. Shortly afterwards, Torsvan/Croves disappeared from Acapulco.

Spota had determined that Croves was Torsvan, but the question "Who is B. Traven?" remained unanswered. For me, the clue to Traven's identity as still another man, Ret Marut, was provided by Manfred George, a German magazine editor. In 1947, George reported that Eric Mühsam, the anarchist poet who participated in the Bavarian revolution, had compared Marut's style to the novels by Traven and concluded that they were written by the same man.

I thought that perhaps in his old age, Traven might no longer want to maintain his anonymity. Furthermore, if he really had been the iconoclastic writer Marut, I believed he would be curious about an equally iconoclastic modern German writer. I sent "Hal Croves" a letter requesting an interview with "Traven," and included an interview I had had with Rolf Hochhuth, author of *The Deputy*.

I didn't realize until many months later to what an extent Traven must have responded. Reading *Der Ziegelbrenner,* I saw that Marut might well have been an intellectual forefather of Hochhuth's, so alike are their attitudes to *Der Stellvertreter* (German for "deputy" or "representative"). Marut repeatedly referred with contempt to those "representatives of Christ" who prayed for victory rather than peace in World War I, just as Hochhuth later condemned the silence of the Pope toward the Nazi persecution of the Jews.

**Cinematographer Gabriel Figueroa Talks About *Rosa Blanca* and the Smell of Oil and Politics**

There was no response from Croves to my letter before I left for Mexico City. While there, I interviewed Gabriel Figueroa, a world-famous cinematographer, an old friend of Croves' and a first cousin of former Mexican president Adolfo López Mateos. He was rather reluctant to talk about *Rosa Blanca,* his potentially explosive film, but was obviously proud of the work.

In the film adaptation of Traven's work, Figueroa had carried out a suggestion by López Mateos, who was then president, that the film go beyond the time of the novel to the historic date of March 18, 1938, when President Lazaro Cardenas courageously decreed the expropriation of Mexican oil fields from their American, Dutch and British owners. López Mateos, who was planning the nationalization of electrical power, may have wanted to remind the Mexicans of the tremendous popularity of the oil expropriation. It is still a mystery whether internal Mexican politics kept *Rosa Blanca* from release at that time or whether its suppression was due to a changing economic relationship between Mexico and the United States—or both.

I was told that López Mateos' successor, President Diaz Ordaz, had called *Rosa Blanca* "the best picture ever made in Mexico" when he was still head of the Interior Department, which houses the Bureau of Film Censorship. Moya Palencio, the censor I interviewed in 1964 believed the film was not released because it was too favorable to Cardenas and "too violent against the U.S." When I spoke with him, he said he had not seen the film and would like to, "but it's a closed case." The government had bought up part of the film industry, shared in production costs, and now owns the film. It was not released until after Traven's death.

When I returned to San Francisco from Mexico, a letter from Croves was waiting. "I will not be able to arrange a meeting with B. Traven," he had written, "because at the moment he is traveling

**50**

in the tropical regions of southern Mexico and surely will not be back within many months. I'm very sorry that I cannot be of help to you in this matter, at least not at present. As soon as you arrive in Mexico City, please send me a note informing me of the name of your hotel at which you're stopping and your room number so that I can get in contact with you. Fact is I'm really eager to meet you. Even if I should not be able to comply with all your wishes, there are so many things in Mexico to see and to learn that you may be assured that your trip will turn out to be an unforgettable one. With best wishes, Sincerely yours, H. Croves.''

Traven Denies That His Books Were
Written in German, but Then
Changes His Story

I thought that Croves' letter indicated a willingness to talk about the past that had so long been shrouded in secrecy, but I was soon to learn otherwise when Croves again agreed to see me in May of 1966. When Rosa Elena Luján picked me up at my hotel, she introduced herself as "Mrs. Croves." A charming, chic woman in her early fifties with dark *sympatico* eyes, she was warm and friendly, and told me how surprised she had been when her husband answered my letters.

I was the first reporter her husband had ever consented to see, and when he slowly walked out on the patio to greet me, the atmosphere was thick with apprehension.

His sudden outburst urging me to forget the man and to think only of his work broke the tension. He began what became a recurrent theme in our interviews: the importance of *what* is written, not the personality of the writer.

"There have been writers who became world-famous writing not about the persons but about the ideas of other writers," he said. "Who was that writer in the 18th century who wrote about Samuel Johnson? Boswell. He became famous writing about Johnson's ideas."

As the sun left the patio where we had been talking, we walked through the comfortable living room hung with paintings into the first floor library—one of four in the house. It was lined from floor to ceiling with books, including all of Traven's novels, which have been published in about 500 editions in 36 languages. Prints of the Mexican Revolution hang on the walls; there is a Diego Rivera sketch of a frog crying *"Chelena"* (Mrs. Croves' nickname), and a bronze casting of the clasped hands of the author and his wife.

The novelist, always carefully maintaining his identity as Hal Croves, started to describe "what I might call the fundamental ideas of Traven. He is against anything which is forced upon human beings including communism or Bolshevism. Let the people decide we want this or we want that. Not like the way Bolshevism was forced upon the

52

Russians. You know he hasn't said so but he considers that communism has brought more unhappiness into the world before the word communism was ever thought of. Some workers think, 'We're happier now because we eat better.' But even in Russia, they have to buy wheat from the States. In the end, Russia loses, because all the gold is given to us because they can't feed their own people. Russia under the Czarist regime exported wheat. Germany lived on Russian wheat.

"You've heard of the Ukraine?" he asked me. I was puzzled by the question but more surprised by his response when I said my parents had been Russian Jews. "Congratulations!" he exclaimed. "I love all people who grew up in Poland and Russia and emigrated. The Israelis [sic] are persecuted in Russia as badly now as in the Czarist regime. They lived as happily under the Czar. What is communism good for if you are slapped on the mouth like those two writers [Sinyavsky and Daniel]? Russia is going to the dogs. No, going to the dogs is too honest. What is communism good for if it also had anti-Semitism like the Nazis?

"Here comes the point about the Nazis," he went on. "Do you know why the Germans yelled all over the world that B. Traven is a German? They yelled all over the world that a great new writer has come into German literature. They needed someone. Many talented young writers never came back from the First World War. The most read writers in pre-war Germany were believed to be Jews. The best. The most read," said Croves. He emphasized that he had no *personal* knowledge of this fact: "I had no contact with Germans at that time."

He said that Traven's first publisher, the Büchergild Gutenberg, founded by the Printers' Union, was German, but published American and French authors almost exclusively. He denied that Traven's books were written in German. (Later that inner man, who hates the lies of this world and demolishes them in his writing, told his wife he regretted lying to me about this.)

In Traven's first correspondence with his publisher, he had insisted upon complete anonymity, forbidding the publication of any personal publicity. When *The Death Ship* appeared in Germany in 1926, Croves told me, "The Germans said, 'Now we have got a German Jack London.' About 1932 when the Nazis were just in the beginning of coming up in power, they accused the Book Guild, 'Why do you publish only foreign authors? Why not publish German writers like Traven?' They threatened the guild and got their storm troopers out.

**53**

"The storm troopers occupied the Book Guild on the pretext that they didn't publish German writers, writers for the *Volk*, writers for the *pueblo*. Actually, it was a kind of business jealousy. On the day Traven was informed the storm troopers had occupied the Book Guild, he sent a letter: 'I hereby prohibit you to publish any of my books. You are not the Book Guild I sent my books to be translated and published. The contract is null and void. I refuse to let the Nazis get a profit.' But the Nazis had published great announcements about selling Traven's books to Russia, and they needed the money for their later invasion. They wrote, 'Recall this letter,' but Traven refused to do it."

The Supreme Court of Germany thereupon fined Traven 2000 gold marks for every day he would not allow the books to be published in Germany.

"So Traven did not get any money. This was in punishment for taking the rights away. All his money, which was in the treasury of the Book Guild, they kept. He didn't get a cent. Today those German royalties owed to Traven are the property of the state.

"If you have followed the story of Germany," Croves continued, "a man by the name of Goering—the second man after that man Hitler—burned all the books, the books the Germans should not read, and when the Nazis invaded Hungary, Czechoslovakia, Yugoslavia and other countries, one of the first orders they gave was that all of the books written by Traven had to be taken out of the bookstores and burned. The booksellers were fusilladed in Belgrade. It should be understood he was not considered Israeli, Traven. They didn't think he had Jewish microbes. But they didn't like his tendency against the state, that the state was a tyrant. That's the point. The Nazis did not include him among the Jewish writers. In this respect, he was o.k. He was just hated. Just as the Russians do now, the Nazis punished those writers who did not follow the party line.

"When all this happened, Traven wrote a new book, *General from the Jungle*. That book did not find a publisher in Germany. They were afraid. The representative of Traven in Switzerland sold it to a publisher in Amsterdam in 1940. It had no sale. Then the Nazis invaded Holland. The whole edition was sold out in one week—maybe 5000 copies. The Nazi soldiers bought the book because they were—how do you call it—Traven admirers.

"In 1926, the Book Guild had asked Traven, 'Won't you please write us a few lines about your life? Just a little biography.' "

But "just a little biography" was exactly what Traven could not supply and so he developed a reason for his anonymity.

"The way I can remember it now," Croves said, "Traven answered the publishers, 'A writer should never be asked for his biography because he is liable to lie to appear more interesting than in fact he is. Just to make himself more readable.' That's the way I get it. 'Actually the writer is of no importance whatever. Anyone who works in your publishing house is just as important in bringing out the books as the writer is'—that was his idea. 'I don't feel myself important enough that my biography should be published.' "

"A writer should be read, not known," Croves said. "So this also applies to the philosophy of Traven: 'In my books you will find my whole personality.' "

He charged that this statement had been misinterpreted by Charles Miller who wrote the "authorized" introduction to *The Night Visitor*. Miller said the books by Traven were autobiographical.

Croves stated, "That is not true. What Traven meant was that you would not find his life in his books, but his thinking and personality. I think that is a very important thing. Any writer should be published to be read and that includes Hemingway. Any writer. You have heard about writers who write one line and insist that it has to be on the front page. Traven is not that kind. He doesn't want any publicity. That is why his books are not known as well as other writers. Do you known how he came in contact with Knopf? At first, he was apparently too much to the left. Knopf had a representative in London, Postgate. He wrote to Knopf, 'Here in Europe is a writer coming up fast who is taking readers by storm.' So Knopf said, 'Get me that man. Get me that writer.' The Curtis Brown agency contacted Traven and this way Knopf published the first book. Knopf announced he would also publish forthcoming books—*Government* and *Carreta*— but he did not. Traven wrote him a letter that was published all over. Traven said, 'You can get the rights on condition you don't make any publicity about the books. Publish as much as you want but not about me. That's my private affair.' We've got to say this about Knopf, he did stick by that promise. He did not even advertise. That's why the American sale was lousy. Though Traven is considered in Europe a millionaire.

"Traven is poorer today than when the first book was published. Up to the time the Nazis came to power, he had a great account at the Book Guild and several banks. Actually even today, in spite of all the noises made about him," Croves said, "he is a poor man. You know it. We know it. It was actually that man Wieder [his Swiss agent], who kept him alive in a certain way when he had nothing to eat. He wrote a pitiful letter to Wieder who sent him a few francs.''

I asked why he did not file suit to recover his German royalties.

"He never tried. Just to avoid the publicity. Who would have believed him? Now the Nazis are out of power. I have been told everyone is against the Nazis today in Germany. No one ever wants to admit he was a Nazi. They all love the Jews. They never had anything to do with the Nazis. That's why Traven never sues. Publicity again. All the publicity about Traven, 'the writer no one knows' and such nonsense,'' Croves said.

The "mystery" about Traven was created by newspapermen, Croves declared. "Today if you don't know what to write and you're starving, write in six hours, here's the cash! Hundreds of newspapermen are riding to fame on the shoulders of that mystery man.''

# 15 "Rosa Blanca, of Thee I Sing, Of Thee, White Rose, Pillar of Peace"

When we met again, Croves came into the library carrying a "very special" bottle of vodka, distilled by Russian immigrants in Mexico and prepared with orange peel. We drank it straight; it was delicious. Croves looked pleased at my enjoyment, but when I asked how it was made, he laughed mischievously and said, "That's another mystery!"

The thought of a mystery reminded him of *Rosa Blanca*. "It is a very good picture," he said, "a great picture. That's why we don't understand why it isn't shown, but what can I do?

"The strangest thing about it is that no one knows and no one tells why it is not permitted in Mexico," Croves said. "Mexico needs exports. Here is an item which can bring in money from England, France, Germany, the United States. Wherever hard money is. You have seen how many editions of the novel there are. It is known in 20 countries."

Although one of the stars of *Rosa Blanca* is Christine Martell, a former Miss France, and now the wife of Miguel Alemán Jr., son of the former president, "even Alemán could do nothing," Croves said. "It means only that no one could do anything about it. This story about the picture in my opinion is almost as good as the book."

As a novel, *Rosa Blanca* has been unable to find a publisher in the U.S. Hill and Wang and a successor, the Lawrence Hill Publishing Company, have reissued other Traven books, but turned down *Rosa Blanca* because the capitalist seemed like a character out of the proletarian novels of the '30s.*

"There is a misunderstanding about *Rosa Blanca*," Croves pointed out. "Perhaps BT meant to explain to the American public what we call here the petroleum problem. The way I see it, it is not

---

*Hill subsequently reconsidered and as this book goes to press is having a new translation made from the original German.

57

the meaning of the book. The true idea, what I feel Traven wanted to show when the owner of the hacienda was threatened with confiscation, is that human beings of today are all industrialized. *I'm* an outsider on all of this. I can judge it independently. *He* wanted to express the value of the soil. That's why no American will understand this (or Mexicans don't understand what Traven wanted to expose: that you can't buy or sell land).

"Anyone who reads it now, especially the Americans, must think, 'That man is crazy!' " He turned to his wife. "Do you think I'm crazy?" "No," she reassured him. "You're perfectly all right."

When Don Jacinto refuses a large offer of gold from the American oilman Collins for purchase of his hacienda, modern readers must think he is insane, Croves said. He repeated parts of the dialogue from the novel, adding, "You can't eat gold. You can't eat money, even if you put money into the ground to grow. The only real thing is earth. Earth is eternal. Gold is not eternal. Gold is at best timely. As long as there is a sun in heaven, earth will produce."

The American lawyer who is trying to buy the land for Collins can't understand this, said Croves, "because he lives in a country where a farm is merchandise. Few Americans of our time want to buy land to have a home and live there. They want to live in the city with TV, opportunity, the radio, and all that. Traven likes to see birds sing in the morning, trees misting in the morning." He said that Charles Miller, a student of Traven, "actually came near the meaning of Traven's books when he said that Traven's 'fundamental idea is like Thoreau's.' "

He recited a poem which appears in the British edition of *Rosa Blanca* but which is, he said, "more beautiful in German."

> Rosa Blanca, of thee I sing,
> Of thee, White Rose, pillar of peace.
> In a world of greed,
> Hypocrisy, graft and felony
> Thou wast not allowed to be.
> Of thee, Rosa Blanca, I sing.

His voice broke as he spoke of "a pillar of peace" and tears appeared in his eyes as he quoted lines from the German edition. "Every day the birds are singing—how you were created by God Almighty. I myself have someday to fall into ashes, but you, Rosa Blanca, will live for ever and ever. My last breath will be my goodbye kiss for you." Tears rolled down his cheeks.

"It is not just a story of petrol," he insisted. "It is what the soil means to poor farmers. Don Jacinto picks up two handfuls of soil and looks at it and begins to cry as if to say that it is God Himself. God has personified Himself in that handful of soil. I hope you understand why all the time we are coming back to *Rosa Blanca*. That doesn't mean the story, but the philosophy. That's in all Traven's books. *Rosa Blanca* comes out easiest to explain."

I asked if the hacienda actually existed and again, he was caught up in caution and the struggle with his double identity. "I don't know. There are thousands of haciendas. It was conceived and written under the dictatorship of Diaz when owners of haciendas were always afraid the *jefes* would take their land away and they had no defense. They had no protection. Whenever they had a piece of land, they had a fear that tomorrow they would not have it. Mexicans take another view of their land. It's really their home. If you take away their home, there is no longer a possibility to be alive. This nearness to the soil," he said, "is the most frequent and most important element in Traven's books."

I asked how he accounted for that. Again, the note of caution entered his voice. "In the first place, I'm sure he was born and brought up on a farm but with little money, a very run-down farm in which Scandinavian immigrant farmers could invest. That's *my* idea. I guess I read that he was born on a run-down farm, *but that's an idea not a fact* [my italics]. I would never classify Traven as an intellectual. He is so very close to earth as an intellectual never can be and never will be."

He asked his wife, "What do you think is the best book by Traven," adding, "but of course you are prejudiced."

"Of course I'm prejudiced," she said. "*Rosa Blanca.*"

Speaking of the *Rosa Blanca* film reminded him of José Kohn who produced three films based on Traven's novels. Kohn, a Czech who had survived the Nazi concentration camps, came to Mexico as a peddler and built up enough assets to enter the motion picture business.

"I'll tell you a wonderful story about what a fine man Joe Kohn is," Croves said. "He came here to do all the books by B. Traven. Sitting in his car, I said, 'Look here, Mr. Kohn. The Nazi regime by now is over. You realize, you read papers, there is still a little bit of feeling left in the world against the Semites, the Jews. You call your pictures José Kohn productions. Everyone knows who you are. Many people will boycott you because of your name. Why not avoid this? Use another fancy name. 'Oh no, I want people to know who I am,' he said. That's the kind of person José Kohn was!''

I felt uneasy as he told this story, but months later, having tried to understand his point of view in *Der Ziegelbrenner,* I thought I knew what the anecdote represented. I believe he was testing Kohn to see if he was motivated by profits or principles. Kohn passed his test.

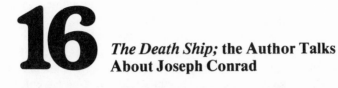

# 16

## *The Death Ship;* the Author Talks About Joseph Conrad

Mrs. Croves reminded her husband that it was time for dinner. He looked at her fondly and said she had almost literally pulled him back from death a few years ago when he was very ill. "They wanted to bring a coffin and take me off and she said, 'If you do it, I will accuse you of first degree murder.' I'm not talking about Traven," he said carefully. "I'm talking about myself."

Later, I told him how I admired *The Death Ship.* He looked at me strangely and said, "If I told you what I think of *The Death Ship,* Traven would kill me." His wife smiled and shook her head. "No, you know he's not like that."

Noting that writers always have favorites among their books, he said cheerfully, "I am not a great writer. I'm just a scriptwriter." He was in fine spirits and eager to talk about the meaning of Traven's books.

"When the reader reads a book by BT, he thinks what does he mean by this phrase? It seems obvious. But there is something between the lines. The deeper idea of *The Death Ship.* It would take me hours to write it down and get my own ideas. It's not just the story of an American sailor. It has a deeper meaning. It's not only about passports. It's that human beings under modern conditions are forced. . . . If you have no passport, you can't return to the idea of the human soul and the human being has been lost entirely. In such lines as I now tell you, we come to the fundamental idea on which the book is based. The American consul says, 'How do I know who you are? You haven't got a birth certificate.' 'You see me, I must be alive,' Gales answered. 'Yes, I see you, but if I report you to Washington, there is no proof.' Gales says, 'Perhaps you even deny that I am alive.' 'Officially, I deny your existence. Officially, you are not alive.' "

That was the fundamental idea, Croves said. "But here comes something else, more between the lines. This is *my* feeling. The

American sailor is not the real important character. The real character is Stanislav. He lost his country during the war. He was innocent of that. He was not even a soldier."

In *The Death Ship*, Traven wrote: "His true name, which, together with his story, I never betrayed to anybody on the *Yorikke*, was Stanislav Koslovski. He was born in Poznan, which then was the capital of the Prussian province of Poznan, or, as it was called by the Prussians, Posen." Stanislav ran away from home rather than become a tailor's apprentice, and he had an incredible series of adventures. Meanwhile the fortunes of war made Poznan a part of Polish territory and Stanislav became another seaman unable to establish his citizenship and forced to work on the death ships.

Croves said he first realized the importance of Stanislav when he saw the film *The Death Ship* in 1959 in Berlin (where, incidentally, his hotel registration carried the name "Croves, also known as Torsvan," as well as his wife's birth date, April 6, 1915.)

Horst Buchholz, who starred as Gales was "awfully good-looking," Croves said. "The hero for the feminine part of the audience. When the picture ran on, Gales disappeared. There grew up like a god the man who played the Pole. He grew up like the greatest hero; he became bigger and bigger. When it was all over what applause he got! It came into my mind that the book is written about that man, not the American sailor. If you read it as I did sitting in the jungle in lonely nights. . . . There came entirely new ideas into my mind. Certain meanings are not as they were written. The meaning of the books, not just the titles. I feel the titles want to lead you away from the true philosophy of Traven. Not intentionally, but that's his spiritual instinct. He doesn't want to expose his soul so he hides it between the lines. His greatness is not only in the tale but between the lines."

The theme of the soil as the only eternal value even appears in *The Death Ship*, Croves pointed out. "One of the sailors says, 'I'm sick of the high seas. I would like to buy me a piece of land.' Even on the high seas and always he thinks of the land!"

Tears appeared in his eyes again and he apologized for becoming emotional.

His wife interrupted to ask, "Are you tired, darling?" "No," he replied vigorously. "I'm very much alive." He wanted to mention that a shipping company executive once wrote to the London *Times* about *The Death Ship*: "This is the truest sea story I have ever read."

"About the *work*, it *is* true! He should have known!," said Croves. "Many have said it beats all the Conrad sea stories."

"In *The Death Ship,* Traven referred to Conrad as a 'certain writer about sailors who are always looking under skirts.' Conrad never mentioned the ones who did the work," Croves criticized. "O'Neill also wrote a play where the lady wants to see the stokehold. And the sailors stand looking under the skirts."

"Well, sailors are sailors," I said.

"Of course," he laughed. "They do it all over the world. It's really normal, but it's not necessary to mention. Still in a way, it has to be mentioned in a book or play. That's the fun."

I asked him to explain his feelings about Conrad. He replied, "I like *Lord Jim.* It's been so long since I read it, I don't want to give an opinion. Conrad was a great writer. Just consider he was born in Poland and wrote such great novels in English! For that I admire the man. The difference between the two writers, in my opinion, is that Conrad wanted just to write good *novels,* entertaining novels. Traven always wanted to write *books.* They came out novels perhaps more accidentally. Some novels don't make you happy as novels. Conrad told a straightforward story which, in my opinion Traven doesn't. That might be why books by Traven may last longer than books by Conrad. They have already forgotten about Conrad. I think Traven will last longer."

In some countries, he said, *The Death Ship* is already considered a classic. "Here is a wonderful item about *The Death Ship,* something 100 per cent Traven in it. When Gales is in the Port of Spain fishing, he gets a big fish and takes pity on it and throws it back. And comes a customs officer who says, 'But it seems to be a very good fish.' Gales replies, 'The fish may have nibbled at a dead sailor.' In fact, Traven *means* to say he told the fish, 'You go back to your mate and be happy. *I* want to be free and so I love freedom, so the fish does also.' This love for animals is in every book."

I told him about a story by Han Suyin who had gone to visit her family in Peking during the Chinese Communist campaign to kill sparrows because they were eating the wheat while people were starving. Dr. Suyin was revolted by the destruction of the birds, but later, on her way through India, she saw sacred cows being kept alive while thousands of people died of hunger. It was a lesson in comparative humanity that she could not forget.

Croves considered the question of India and the sacred cows and said, "We come over to Western ideas of cruelty. I don't know how you personally feel about meat, but human beings can live entirely on vegetables. We don't do it, but it can be done. Who is more important on earth? The human being? Because *He* wrote it in the Bible that all animals had to be *His* slaves? But ask God what He actually meant. He created the animals. They're just as important as the human being. It's just my *personal* opinion. I myself would say I'm not sure if the human being is of so much more value than an animal.''

Later that evening, his own basic care for both people and animals was apparent. His stepdaughter, Malu, 22, one of Señora Lujan's two daughters by her first husband, Carlos Montes de Oca, drove us to a Chinese restaurant and left to visit her sister, Rosa Elena, 23. Malu, a pert and vivacious young woman, affectionately kissed her stepfather, calling him ''Skipper,'' and said she would pick us up later. Mrs. Croves mentioned that the parrot, Caroline, also calls him ''Skipper.'' With a sardonic look, Croves commented, ''The parrot calls me by my *right* name, *Burro*.'' He translated so that I could not miss the point. ''Jackass.''

While dogs like to meddle in the affairs of men, B. Traven points out in *The Treasure of the Sierra Madre,* ''Burros are less interested in men's personal doings, they mind their own business. That's the reason why donkeys are thought to have a definite leaning about philosophy.''

It was the first of many dinners with the Croves in which I felt alternately awkward—because his deafness usually left him out of the conversation—and touched by their affection for each other. As we prepared to leave the table, he asked for a *bolsa* for ''crisps'' for Caroline. Mrs. Croves looked embarrassed, but he went adamantly about his business of collecting scraps for the parrot. In the car, he dug into his pocket, a repository for many little goodies, pulled out an almond cookie for Malu and placed it in her mouth. ''Good?'' he asked her tenderly.

When they left me at my hotel he said warmly, ''Don't be surprised, one of these days, we might just burst in at your office and say, 'Where is that Miss Stone?' '' He kissed me goodbye and admonished pleadingly, ''Don't write anything that might hurt us.'' He smiled shyly and they left.

# 17

## He Insists on His Identity as Hal Croves; a Long Story About an Old Friend

On that first visit to Mexico I had not asked Croves directly if he were B. Traven; I didn't want to put him in the undignified position of lying. I assumed he would discuss it when and if he were ready. Although I love a mystery as much as the next person, in this case I had not set out to be a detective or even to engage in the kind of questioning that goes into a routine job of reporting. I knew there were painfully complicated reasons for his long silence, and I hoped that he might open up without any aggressive probing. I was therefore surprised to learn, when I returned to Mexico to visit Traven again in November 1966 that *Siempre* magazine had just published what was, purportedly, "the first interview with B. Traven." There were a few glimpses of the household, photographs of the living room stairway and a sculptured bust of Traven (Hal Croves) by his friend Federico Canessi, the usual "authorized American history of the author who is now a Mexican citizen," and the rumor that he was the son of "Kaiser Wilhelm II or a Duke of Bavaria." The interview had been given *on condition* that the name Croves be omitted from the story, the reporter, Luis Suarez, subsequently revealed.

Despite the *Siempre* report and one based on it in the *New York Times,* the writer continued to insist on his identity as Croves during our conversations. I spent the next month in a state of irritation and frustration, waiting for scattered appointments with him. Whenever I did get to see him, I sensed the conflict between his friendliness toward me and his regret that he had ever agreed to see a reporter.

However, our first dinner engagement at a favorite German restaurant, the Bellinghausen, was amiable. The Croves were greeted by some friends, including a young woman, the daughter of artist Orozco Romero. Her strong and intelligent face showed an amazing resemblance to the late Esperanza López Mateos, sister of the former Mexican President and Traven's friend and translator.* Croves, who

---

*Miss López Mateos, I later learned, was a strong-minded, courageous and politically

**65**

had been looking intently at her, quietly asked his wife if she had noticed the similarity to Esperanza. "That's a long story," he said. "It would take many hours to tell."

Croves seemed to wrench himself back across the years, turned his attention again to his wife and said, "Did I tell you I still love you today? See what a little good food will do?" It was the authentic voice of Traven, a little irony always sharpening the soft edge of his tenderness. But when Mrs. Croves laughed about the effect of food on his affections, he was disturbed and assured her that he had meant what he said. Across the table, Mrs. Croves told me softly that she had first met him when she was a young girl, but didn't have enough sense to marry him then. They were finally married in San Antonio, Texas, in 1957, following her divorce from her first husband, a light-hearted businessman whose beliefs were completely different from her own.

---

militant woman who was considerably to the left of her brother, Adolfo. She was a woman of many interests, a linguist, editor of a medical journal and a cave explorer. At one time, she had been married to Robert Figueroa, Gabriel Figueroa's brother. She played an important part in reviving interest in Traven's books and getting them published in Mexico. After Miss López Mateos committed suicide in 1951, Señora Luján, who had helped her on the Spanish translation of *The Rebellion of the Hanged,* continued her work as Traven's agent and translator.

# 18 "Be Careful How You Handle the Subject of Religion"

Still carefully maintaining his separate identity, Hal Croves told me that sometimes it takes many years even for him to understand the full meaning of Traven's books. He cited "Macario," which had been selected by Martha Foley as one of the best short stories in 1954, and which was then made into a prize-winning film. It is about the dream of a poor Mexican woodcutter whose heart's desire is to have a whole roasted turkey all to himself. When his wife finally surprises him with this treat and he sits alone in the woods, savoring the anticipated pleasure, he is importuned to share it by a devil disguised as a *charro* (costumed horseman), Our Lord in the guise of a pilgrim and Father Time as the Bone Man. Macario can shrewdly hold his own with the first two, but like the rest of us, he cannot outwit Father Time.

" 'Macario' has a certain line which no one has discovered," Croves said. "It was discovered only in Czechoslovakia. An idea. Macario sits there with the turkey. Then comes the pilgrim and says, 'I'm hungry. Just give me a bite.' He refuses.

"Then comes in the critic of the Czech newspaper. Look at the irony of that man Traven. He tells later to the devil 'how could I with my unclean hands give a piece of turkey to the Lord? Besides He whose Father owns the whole world, who created all the animals, He could get all the *pavos,* that Man who worked so many miracles. Why does He come to me; He comes like a poor *campesino* and asks for part of the turkey—that Man who, if He wants to, can command all the animals.'

"No one ever detected the irony except that Czech critic." He said he now realized "for Traven, the pilgrim represented the Church. And the Church is always asking for the last penny. Not just the pilgrim, the Church."

He warned me to be careful about how I handled the subject of religion. "You known how the American public likes religion. In

*Land of Springtime,* there is a line. I guess it wouldn't hurt anyone if you tell this. We fell for that story about Paradise. God told Adam and Eve not to take an apple. Then finally they gave up Paradise just for an apple. Tell that to a Mexican Indian, he would never believe someone would give up Paradise for an apple. You'd have to make it at least a mango!''

"Dear Judy, you don't know the history of Mexico. They had a far better religion than we have got. When we talk of Paradise, we think it is a wonderful place where we can sing hymns. A wonderful life of no work and you get your eats and drinks. Do you know the Paradise of the Aztecs? Traven has explained it somewhere also in the course of a story. Once the Aztecs had to work harder in Paradise than on earth because even among Indians today they cannot live without work. They had to keep busy even in Paradise. They had to shape the clouds, guide the lightning; they had to paint the flowers and guide the butterflys. There was no sleeping or drinking or good French wine! It is in *Land of Springtime.*"

He said he didn't want *Land of Springtime,* his travel book, published in English now because it is out of date. "Traven wrote this before the Revolution. Whole chapters would have to be changed. You don't know the changes that have taken place since the Revolution. What you see now in Mexico City didn't exist. The only big hotel when Traven first came here was the Hotel Regis. The highest building was only four stories high. The general standards of health have improved immensely. When Traven came to Mexico you found hardly anyone who could read or write. Now it is the other way around. In this way, the Revolution has done very well.

"When Traven came, people from the puebla were in rags and hungry. You don't see them any longer. The only decently dressed people you saw at that time were in the Protestant churches. In the Catholic churches, the poor came as dirty as when they left their beds or dirtier still. It's interesting to note how the churches have influenced them. The highest figure of educated people among democratic people who can read and write are the Scandinavians. In Germany or Central Europe, those sections under Catholic influence have no reading or writing. Here in Mexico, when a girl wanted to go to school, the padre went to the father or mother and said, 'You don't let that girl go to school. What does she want to learn writing for? She will only write to her *novio* [sweetheart]; she will only read bad books.' "

And he wasn't sure that he wanted people to read Traven's last book, *Aslan Norval.* "He thinks he can do better. I don't think it is a book that should go by the name BT in my personal opinion."

In Germany the book was criticized for its "emphasis" on sex: Aslan has an affair with a young, disillusioned Korean war veteran and realizes the she prefers her much older husband.

"The book," said Croves, "is too sexy and not even very well written in the sexy idea. I would never write that book in the way it's written. The way Traven wrote it, it is about a woman who wants a lover. I don't understand why he wrote that book. It seems to have been written involuntarily." ("I do not control the stylus, it is guided by someone else who only uses my dull, ponderous hand," wrote Ret Marut in *Der Ziegelbrenner*. I thought that *Aslan* was about as sexy as the *Ladies Home Journal*.)

I mentioned that the East Germans believe the book is a forgery. "I would say it's not in the style of Traven," he replied. "It's not his way of writing."

His wife added that critics have said he should stop writing about the Indians. "It was in the time of *Lolita* and he wanted to put sex in the book, but it's not his way. *Aslan* is copyrighted in our name [Luján and Croves]. That's why some people say it's not by Traven. We hope to get two new books from Traven soon."

He was in such a good mood that I told him how much I had enjoyed his humorous story, "Foreign Correspondent." In it, a young would-be reporter is discouraged from pursuing a journalistic career after he files a story from Mexico about six bloody heads: five army officers and one "goddamned American newspaper correspondent," impaled on iron spikes by Pancho Villa's orders. I was rewarded for my compliment with a twinkle and I suddenly realized that, although all writers crave an audience, this was one of the rare times when he had met a Traven fan face to face.

This set off what I then thought was a spontaneous stream of recollections about the time "Traven was held a prisoner of Villa because he was a writer, a snooper." I later wondered if the whole point of the story—and perhaps, our conversation—was to mislead Traven "snoopers," including myself, by indicating that the writer was in Mexico in 1915 and not in Germany. The short story, under the German title "A Truly Bloody Story," was inserted in a 1957 German edition of *In the Bush* and is the only one with an indication of time. It appeared at a period when the German press was filled with speculation about Traven's identity and when Traven wanted no part of Germany. I read later that Villa had been friendly to John Reed and other American correspondents in 1914, and I wondered if

**69**

the Mexican general would have changed his attitude so drastically in one year. Was Traven projecting his own feelings about the press on Villa, or was he telling the story of someone he knew who may have been a prisoner of Villa? There is evidence that Traven, as Ret Marut, was still an actor in Germany in 1915.

### Traven Talks of His Books, His Admiration for Pancho Villa, and His Work with John Huston

It was an unfortunate day. Croves was still suffering from a cold, and he was irritable because the maid had uprooted one of his plants. But his mood lifted temporarily after he had some soup and greeted a visitor, Igal Maoz, a young Israeli artist. Maoz had first heard of Traven when the people on his kibbutz sang the song from *The Cotton Pickers*. It has been set to music by Hans Eisler and became popular in pre-Hitler Germany. Maoz happily sang the Hebrew version for us. In the British edition, translated by Eleanor Brockett, it begins:

> Cotton is worn by king and princeling
> Millionaire and president,
> But the wretched cotton-picker
> Hardly gets a ruddy cent ...

Maoz presented the "skipper" with a Van Gogh print of a sail-boat and left. Croves wandered off restlessly and finally appeared with an exquisite white orchid. He presented it to me gallantly and said, *"Una orquídea para una orquídea."* For the first time, I had written down a few questions, and handing him the paper, I felt somewhat abashed at the unfair exchange. He put on his reading glasses, scanned the questions and declared with heavy irony, "This is an *interview!* The *New York Times* said 'No more interviews!' "

Asked whether a writer should participate in political action, he answered, "A shoemaker sticks to his shoes, an actor sticks to his profession. Leave politics to the professional politicians. Traven would never participate in any manifestation with placards or what do you call them? Because he definitely sticks to his work. He has very little time to participate in any demonstrations no matter what the movement."

In the hope that he might finally drop the role of Croves with me and begin to discuss the true background of the books, I asked if Stanislav in *The Death Ship* was based on a real person. Most readers have always assumed that *The Death Ship* was a fictionalized account of Traven's own escape from Germany. My hopefully subtle efforts to start him talking were no match for his barricades, even though at times I thought he wanted to speak freely.

"I like that question about Stanislav," he said. "You're stealing something from me. I thought of writing about it. Yes, Stanislav was a real person." For a fraction of a second, the curtain opened, and then snapped shut. "*I* didn't know anybody in the books written by BT. How could *I* know Stanislav?

"*The Treasure of the Sierra Madre,* in Croves' opinion, is the real autobiographical novel, whereas all the others are not." A few minutes later, he amended his words slightly. "Only one of all the novels could be classified as a *biographic* novel, not an *auto*biography, but a biographic novel. One of the main characteristics of BT is in it, but let the reader find out who it might be."

I thought that he was deliberately misleading me, but much later, from people associated with the filming of *The Rebellion of the Hanged* in 1954, I heard a rumor that Croves had entered Mexico through Guatemala where he and a companion had found and fought over a "fabulous" burial tomb. Croves was pictured as a complex man—spellbinding with his stories of finding the secret grave of Cuauhtemoc, a location he never revealed; but infuriating, as he angrily defended and insisted upon exact adherence in the film to each detail of the novel because "*that's* the way it happened—I was there with Traven."

With a different eye, I reread *Treasure* and also "The Night Visitor" in which Gales, visited by the ghost of an ancient Aztec prince, finds the prince's tomb and his remains, as well as the golden ornaments of his lifetime. Those golden ornaments represented, not wealth, but the love felt for the prince by those who gave him the trinkets. The gold in *Treasure* represents nothing but greed; the search for gold, the symbol of corruption of men, possessed solely by lust for money. The three partners, Dobbs, Curtin and old Howard, understand, in different ways, how the obsession for gold changes men. Like Traven, who had once had a sizable source of funds in Germany, Howard also had a "bank account" of "over a hundred thousand spot cash" until the cash gave out and he was pushing old friends in the streets of Oso Negro to get 50 centavos for a cot to sleep on; and like Traven, Howard is able to laugh at fate—even when it blows the gold dust to the winds.

Reading down my list of questions, Croves ignored one about a German book which had included Traven in an analysis of American writers, along with Jack London, Sinclair Lewis and Upton Sinclair, and went on to discuss the great figures of the Mexican Revolution.

"Some I don't want to make feel bad," he replied characteristically, "so I don't want to say how Traven feels. For instance I know that Cardenas is a great admirer of Traven. Then we have to study *Land of Springtime* correctly. BT has a great admiration for Calles. He was the builder of the Revolution, the first to start building highways, schools, dam sites. BT thinks Zapata is important. He uses the war cry of Zapata, *'tierra y libertad,'* in his books. Maybe you should cut Calles," he said, perhaps thinking of two diametrically different roles played by Calles in two periods of Mexican history. "You have got to consider," he chided me, "*we* have to live in Mexico. You don't." "Mention Madero. Personally, I—I'm not talking for BT—I admire the most hated revolutionary, Villa."

When I asked exactly when Traven had been a prisoner of Villa, he replied, "When he had time to write. It must have been when he did not bring out any scripts in 1914-15, but of this I am not positive."

My discomfort was suffocating and sensing my reaction, he said, "Since you believe I'm Traven, it's very difficult for me to answer this question. It's a very long story."

He launched into a lengthy, confused attempt to explain why he had adopted the name of Hal Croves in order to keep his hand in on the filming of *The Treasure of the Sierra Madre* without revealing his true identity as its author.

It all began when John Huston wrote a letter to Traven. That letter, he said, "came into the possession of Croves because I am a representative of Traven."

Croves sent Huston a cable asking the director to meet him in Mexico City. "I, Croves, came and visited John Huston and he asked me questions about certain details. I said, 'Here, present it this way.' He agreed. He was even applauding, 'Great ideas, Mr. Croves!'

" 'The ideas I give you are according to the sense of Traven because we talked it over months ago.' " Croves told Huston. " 'You, I and Traven will agree because I know exactly what is on his mind.'

"I worked so well with John Huston that he even put me on the payroll of Warner Brothers. With this it started. If you go to the Churubusco studio here and ask for Traven, they will say they never heard of him. Ask them, 'Do you know Hal Croves?' 'Of course, he worked with us on *Rosa Blanca*!' Even my great friend and translator [Esperanza López Mateos] knew me only by the name of H. Croves.''

Referring to some Traven book copyrights in the name of Croves, he said, ''You have to understand it is impossible for me to separate from Traven. I'm part of it. Even to copyright and translation. I took the responsibility. I was so closely united with BT on the motion pictures. We knew sooner or later all the books would be made into pictures. I couldn't go to Churubusco and say, 'I'm BT'; they'd say I'm a liar. We needed a legal person. In literary history, more than one writer does the same as O. Henry, but everyone knew who he was. HC is the juridical person BT accepted, and the money is paid to me. They know the money goes to the writer. When we sold *Treasure,* people who put up millions had to be sure. There was never a letter from Traven writing to Warner Brothers saying, 'Where's my money?' I mostly sign for and on behalf of BT. It's always accepted. Sometimes the check is made out to BT and he gets it.''

Croves looked old, weary and annoyed. ''Hal Croves would like to write about Traven's books sooner or later, and perhaps he will do it because I think I know more about the books than anyone else. John Huston would say to me, 'You must be Traven.' And I would say, 'Oh, John, leave me alone!'

''Personally I cannot accept to be called Mr. Traven. I have no right to accept that name. Croves is Croves and Traven is Traven. That is fully accepted in Mexico this way. I've got the full rights to act for BT and that's all. Besides, who would gain if I come out and say, 'Yes, I'm B. Traven'? Nothing would be better for the books. Nothing would change the economic situation. People would say, 'Well, one is not true.' ''

I asked if the *Siempre* interview with ''Traven'' and the *New York Times* story about it were lies. ''Not only the *Siempre* article,'' he grumbled. ''Everybody who writes is a liar, photographing the stairway, that's all! You may mention that people who have written about the mystery man have made more money than BT has made so far. Who I admire in all this company is the one who said, 'Why don't they leave that poor man in peace?' What does it matter? The books exist. Does it matter who wrote Shakespeare's plays—Lord Bacon, Lord Fifi, Lord Pipi? No matter who he is, the books will be great books. The most terrific stories have been published about Shakespeare! Why did I ever get mixed up with Traven? I didn't go looking for him. It came to me. Up to the time of the motion pictures, nobody cared about Hal Croves.''

74

I felt depressed and guilty when I said goodnight. With sadness and anxiety, he nodded, saying he trusted me, and I sensed his own guilt and conflict about the conversation that evening.

Later, I recalled his words in *The Death Ship:* "Rarely did anyone give his true name on the *Yorikke.* It is an old rule, only not sufficiently obeyed, but a good rule: If you do not wish to be lied to, do not ask questions! The only real defense civilized man has against anybody who bothers him is to lie. There would be no lies if there were no questions."

I wondered again why I had embarked on this project when the man's deepest need appeared to be the maintenance of his privacy, but *still* I wished he would tell his whole story, complete with his insight into such different periods of world history in Germany and in Mexico. Finally, I wrote a four-page letter, expressing everything I had wanted to say to him. I wrote that I believed Hal Croves was B. Traven and that B. Traven had been Ret Marut; that the origin of the dilemma about his identity went back to the mystery surrounding his parentage; that his flight from execution in Germany compounded the reasons behind his insistence on anonymity for "B. Traven."

Just as Traven sought to understand the lives of the Indians, so, I wrote, he could not blame me for looking for clues to the life of Traven. I thought the basic clue was to be found in *The Death Ship,* in Gales' reply to the consul: " 'Birth registered? I do not know, sir. When this happened, I was too small to remember exactly if it was done or not.' ... 'Was your mother married to your father? ...' 'I never asked my mother. I thought it was her own business and that it concerns nobody else ... How can I prove anything since my birth was not registered? ... My honest name in the register of a death ship? Not me. I have not come down so far yet' ... So I abandoned my good name. I think it was anyway only my mother's name, since it has never been clear if my father had really his name added or not. I severed all family connections. I no longer had a name that was by right my own."

## An Excursion to San José Purua, and Recollections of *The Treasure of the Sierra Madre*

A week passed while I debated giving him the letter; I thought he would be angered, particularly by my first reference to his German past. He had suggested taking a trip to San José Purua where *Treasure* was filmed; I decided to wait and see what happened on that excursion.

It was early in the morning on December 19 when they met me. As usual, the Mexico City sky was grey and oppressive. Croves nodded at me distantly and his wife looked worried. I knew he was accustomed to rising late in the day and working far into the night, so I tried not to take his coolness personally. We stopped at a hotel and changed to a tour limousine. Croves carried what looked like a woman's large handbag stuffed with personal belongings and a small suitcase with an enormous lock. Bitter experience had taught him the necessity of double-locking everything, he said. During the drive, he talked about the history of Mexico City and its growth, the murders committed on the highway, and teased me about taking me across the state line. Finally we passed through a gateway labeled *Poblita Luz Cardenas* and through a stone archway to the hotel, which looked vaguely Japanese with red tiled roofs and red bannisters connecting the passageways to the living units. The setting—a valley surrounded by mountains—was beautiful and lush with yellow ciranda trees, velvety red *noche buena* (poinsetta) bushes, exotic purple and magenta blossoms and both orange and banana trees.

It was Croves' first visit in 20 years and he was silent most of the time. Everything had changed, he said, with the exception of all that chicken on the menu. He recalled a large stag table in the center of the dining room. "Not even Betty Bacall sat there. So the men could talk about things ladies shouldn't hear." Betty was a "fine woman," he had told me earlier when he recalled how she had once saved the crew from the deadly monotony of their diet of "chicken, chicken, chicken every day." She drove to Mexico City one Sunday

76

and returned with a sackful of cans, including Boston baked beans.

I asked if he had liked Bogart; it wasn't exactly a maximum security question.

"Oh yes," he began enthusiastically, then hesitated and said, "Well, I won't say since there's a newspaperwoman here. But yes, I liked him very much." He walked on lost in his thoughts.

His complete withdrawal from conversation was in marked contrast to the day of my first visit with him when he had talked with animation about the filming of *Treasure* and his old quarrel with John Huston about the casting of Walter Huston as Howard, the grizzled prospector.

"I still remember Howard crawling up the mountain. He did it like an old goat. I said, 'John, he is your father, but not the type.' Traven wrote about a man so old he can't even stand on his feet any more but he still has the dream of gold, gold, gold and the gold goes away. Lewis Stone would have been the right type in my idea and I'm sure Traven's. I admit that Walter Huston was great. He deserved the Oscar he received. Lewis Stone would not have been so good. Only he was more like the character Traven had in mind. Hal Croves actually admires John Huston as a director. We often worked on the film until 4:30 in the morning, until we were both falling asleep."

He had once told me that Huston used to needle him, saying, "Come clean, Croves, admit you're Traven and get it over with."

After *Treasure* was completed, Huston had told the press that he believed Croves was Traven, and postulated his own theory of Traven's double identity—"Traven in contact with people disintegrates and becomes ridiculous. And he is intelligent enough to know that he is ridiculous." Croves furiously denied the identification and ordered his agents never to deal with Huston again.

The pain and anger of the postscript to the filming may have been revived again by the sight of San José Purua, causing his retreat into what seemed like hostile silence.

Croves still seemed to want to be alone, so I took a long hike down the mountainside to the river, watched the waterfalls nearby, and wished I would not have to give him that letter. When we met in the evening, he greeted me with a big smile, to my great relief.

Knowing that I had visited Chiapas during the previous week, he talked about his admiration for the primitive tribe of Lacandon Indians which is slowly dying out there.

"They are a free people," he said. "They have never been conquered. They raise tobacco and manage to live in the jungle despite being attacked by wild beasts. I told him the Indians refused to permit their photographs to be taken and wondered how Traven had managed to do so successfully. He said the Indians believe that "Their souls would be taken away if they were photographed."

"Like you," his wife interrupted with a smile.

"It is a belief held by many primitive people," he said. "And Orthodox Jews don't carry their passports, their documents on the Sabbath. It's a good belief," he concluded sympathetically. I did not ask to take his picture.

Later, Mrs. Croves asked, "Would your boss be mad if you don't write a story? My husband said he'd be your friend for life if you don't." Feeling upset, I replied that I had a commitment to fulfill. We drove back to Mexico City in nearly total silence and when I left them, I gave him my letter. That night I decided it would be pointless to prolong my stay in Mexico.

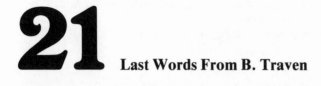

# 21 Last Words From B. Traven

A few days after Christmas I returned to the Croves' home for my last visit. The Christmas tree in the hallway was brightly decorated with gold balls. When Croves came in, he shook hands in a very friendly manner and asked, "'Have you seen what Santa Claus has brought you?" I had mentioned that I like Mexican onyx and they gave me an onyx powder box.

I was surprised when he asked, "When do you go back to the chain gang?" In a severe tone, but only half-joking, I said he should stop discriminating against reporters; it was as bad as any other kind of discrimination. "I'm not against newspapers," he replied seriously. "We can even say we like you very much, but BT *hates* reporters."

"In that letter you wrote," he went on unexpectedly, "that man Marut was a polemical writer. I think he was a political charlatan. He never wrote a poem [later I read his poem in *Der Ziegelbrenner*] and BT has written many. That paper—he didn't even write all of it, some other people wrote it. If he translated Shelley—how did they let him get away with that during the war? Some German newspapermen came here and said they would welcome Marut as a hero. I don't even think he took part in the revolution."

Later, we walked down the Reforma, which is always hung with magnificent lights during the holiday season. As we passed the American Embassy, he mentioned that the building contains an air raid shelter. "I guess they're afraid of demonstrations," he said. Then he thought of that day's dismal news—about the rampaging Chinese "cultural revolution" and the way all fine dreams for the brotherhood of man come to an end—and he shook his head. "No, now it's not the United States they demonstrate against. It's against the Chinese in Russia and against the Russians in China." His disgust was obvious; once he had cared and he still cared enough to feel disgust.

As we drove home, Croves said, "About that letter, I would have to answer it point by point. You will hear from me. For the most part, I thought it was a very good letter."

I kissed him goodbye, feeling very sad, and he said, "We have enjoyed having you. Don't spoil it."

Those were my last words from B. Traven.

# Part Three: Epilogue

**B.** Traven died on March 26, 1969. Those who thought his death might clear up some of the mysteries in his life soon read a new set of obfuscations.

In an Associated Press story from Mexico City, Rosa Elena Luján discussed the will Traven had drawn up three weeks before his death. "My husband hold me to reveal his identity after his death," she told the AP. "We talked about this several times. He felt it would be a great responsibility for me if I attempted to maintain his secret after death. Even in his will, he points out if anyone wants to write a biography about him, I must approve it first." She said that Traven Torsvan was his real name, that he was born in Chicago, Illinois, on May 3, 1890, the son of Burton Torsvan, a Norwegian farmer, and Dorothy Croves, an Englishwoman who soon tired of America and settled in Germany. Later he used the noms de plume of B. Traven, Ret Marut and Hal Croves.

An explanation for the last name was provided in an obituary in the *Los Angeles Times* by William Weber Johnson, who first reported on the Traven mystery for *Life* magazine in 1947. "Hal Croves," he claimed, "was a combination of Traven's mother's maiden name and his Scottish grandfather's given name, Halward. "He was adrift at an early age," Johnson wrote, "went to sea, was shanghaied at least once and went on the beach in Tampico. He returned to Germany and, as Ret Marut, became an actor, writer and editor. ..." Johnson, a scholar and author, presented the widow's information on Traven's birthdate and birthplace as factual without attributing it either to Traven's will or to her. He failed to mention the more likely possibility that Traven's birth date was 1882 or the "rumor" that the author was the illegitimate son of Kaiser Wilhelm II.

Neither Johnson's obituary nor my articles had been totally candid. When we first met in 1967 following the publication of my stories on Traven in *Ramparts,* I told him more about my conversations with Rosa Elena Luján than had appeared in print. At that time, we discussed our ambivalent interests in writing full-scale biographies on Traven. It is time to amend the record.

\* \* \*

During my trip to Mexico in May 1966, before meeting "Croves," I had lunch with his wife. To my surprise, she told me then that Traven's father was "a very high German official, a Hohenzollern." Traven, she said, had learned this from his mother, an "American" singer or actress, when he was in his teens and "already fighting against that man." He could not forgive his mother for telling him about his identity, Lujan said, and "he spoke highly of the man who was his father although he had fought against him." Later, Traven's first words to me were "Forget the man! What does it matter if he is the son of a Hohenzollern prince or anyone else?" Because of the awkward nature of our conversations, I did not press for more specific information about his early years from either of them.

When I returned to Mexico in November 1966, I asked Señora Luján if Kaiser Wilhelm II was the Hohenzollern to whom she had referred and she confirmed it. During the Travens' trip to Germany in 1959 for the premiere of the film *The Death Ship,* Traven, very excited by the old familiar places, told her for the first time about his mother's revelation. Later, he closed the door on that subject. Under the continuing difficulties of interviewing "Croves" I did not see how I could use what his wife had told me, unless he himself disclosed his secret. (Assuming, of course, that his mother *had* told him this story, and that it was true.)

While I was writing my *Ramparts* pieces, *Stern* magazine published Gerd Heidemann's article (April 13, 1967) reporting Señora Luján's statement that Traven was the son of Kaiser Wilhelm II. When I telephoned her in Mexico, she denied making such a statement to Heidemann. I challenged her since she had told me the same thing, but she pleaded with me not to quote her. She said her husband was furious and upset about the *Stern* article with its pictures of Traven, the Kaiser's children and a German woman, Irene Zielke, reputed to be Traven's daughter by Elfriede Zielke, an actress he had known before World War I. Lujan said he was still capable of leaving her, even at his advanced age. In a letter to me, dated June 21, 1967, she wrote about the epochs in Traven's life, adding, "Please do not quote me as having said his mother was a singer or an actress because I haven't. I just hope that after all this noise, he doesn't want to start a fourth epoch and leave everything behind . . . including me . . . Although he loves me and the girls very much (the only woman he ever wanted to marry and did marry) I realize he could still do it again."

And so, I wrote around the subject, partly out a desire to spare Señora Luján any further unhappiness (several people who had worked with "Hal Croves" had told me about his strong, quick temper). I also thought that discretion at that time might strengthen my own future position as a biographer, although I wasn't sure I wanted to undertake this Herculean task. How was it possible for

Traven to have produced such a major body of work for publication in Germany in the first few years after his arrival in Mexico, reputedly in 1923? Was he the *sole* author of all the Traven books? Why is there so much difference in style between *The Treasure of the Sierra Madre* and the other novels? Only a major, objective work of literary detection and scholarship could begin to answer all the questions about his life and work.

After the *Ramparts* articles appeared, Señora Luján repeated the story about the Kaiser to Lawrence Hill, who is now U.S. publisher of Traven's works. When I suggested to Hill that he reprint the *Ramparts* series along with one of Traven's short novels, he looked dubious. He told me that Luján and Traven had been very disturbed about my references to anti-Semitism in Marut's German period. If he were to republish the articles, Hill told me, he would want to eliminate that section. I said I would reject any such censorship and the subject was not pursued.

\*     \*     \*

When I returned to Mexico for Traven's final rites, Señora Luján was cordial as ever but she had little to say about Traven's reactions to my *Ramparts* series. For the first time, she showed me her husband's third-floor study with his most personal books, including the *Almanach de Gotha,* a reference work on European royalty. On the wall were pictures of a bridge across the river Trave in Lübeck, Germany, and a photograph of Kaiser Wilhelm II. (In her introduction to Traven's *The Kidnapped Saint and Other Stories,* published in 1975, Lujan refers to the Kaiser's photograph without further comment. She undoubtedly will have more to say on the subject in the biography she is now preparing.)

Traven, who wrote so often of his scorn for funeral pomp and ceremony, had asked simply that his ashes be scattered over the jungle of Chiapas, for many years his refuge from the world. Before that request could be executed, the state of Chiapas decided to offer its own homage.

On April 18, I flew to Tuxtla Gutierrez, capital of Chiapas, with Señora Luján, her daughter Malu, Traven's friend, the sculptor Federico Canessi, and William Weber Johnson. The scene at the new state university was rich with irony that only BT, the wily old anarchist himself, would have fully appreciated. In the oppressive heat of the day, state officials and local intellectuals, formally attired in un-comfortable-looking black suits and white shirts, paid tribute to the author. His ashes rested in a simple urn of red cedar on a table flanked by two pieces of driftwood, against a dark green velvet back-drop. The platform was banked with lilies and roses. Pretty school girls in their white-and-blue outfits half-filled the small auditorium with its three crystal chandeliers.

The next day, we flew south to Ocosingo (pop. 2500-3000), a village in a valley ringed by mountains at the edge of the Lacandon jungle. A marimba band was on hand to greet Traven's widow and hand-made bamboo *cohetes* (rockets) were sent ringing into the air. I was happy to see at least one mangy dog in attendance—finally, an authentic note for a farewell to Traven. Children who had been given the day off from school happily lined the dirt road, Calle Madero, throwing flowers. One little boy, asked if he knew what the occasion was, proudly replied, "It's a program for Pasteur."

The line of march stopped at the Parque Hidalgo with its pale green church facing the green, orange and yellow town hall at the other end of the square. There two California priests and five San Francisco nuns stationed at the Mission San Jacinto were waiting to observe the unexpected festivities. I asked one of the priests if he knew the history of the heretic they were about to honor. He listened with grave interest, showing both a touch of amusement and gentle respect for the dear departed. Sister Mari Cafferty, who had worked in a nearby clinic for the last five years, told me about the high death rate among children from one to seven years. Most of the youngsters suffered from anemia, TB and malnutrition, she said. Below, in the square, black-braided, neatly dressed little school-girls giggled with excitement.

When night fell, Señora Lujan and Dr. Luis Antonio Gordillo, the municipal president, who was carrying the cedar box, led an eerie procession of several hundred men and women down dark streets, lit only by a lantern, to a home selected as the "most humble" in Ocosingo. All the while, three Indians played hand drums and a kind of pennywhistle. Inside the bare, one-room thatched hut, the urn was placed on a table lit by four candles. For two deeply quiet hours, the black-eyed villagers would enter, one by one, to pay their respects. linger a while and share the sorrow of the widow. It didn't matter who that widow or her husband was; her grief was theirs. Their eyes reflected the sorrow of generations; they were the eyes that a German anarchist had searched and sensed in them a depth of tragedy and humanity unlike anything he had known in the world he left behind.

Then, the spell of silence was broken. It was time to feed the living. Simple tamales wrapped in banana leaves had been cooking over an open fire next door. They were now passed around for all to share. Finally, Rosa Elena, Malu, another friend and I retired to the

**86**

little oblong room we were sharing with an interesting variety of small jungle creatures in what we nicknamed the Ocosingo Hilton. We were worn out by the heat, the heavy emotion and the solemnity, lost in our own thoughts of what Traven would have said about the event, when we heard the quiet strains of the marimba band giving us a midnight serenade.

Malu stood at tiptoe on her cot, peered out through the high window and giggled. There was William Weber Johnson sharing a bottle with the marimba players. He gallantly passed it to us through the window. I could swear I heard the rebel Ret Marut cheer and the strains of Traven's favorite funeral music "taingonnarainnomonomo," the song the Indians played for the death of the child in *The Bridge in the Jungle*. It was a BT finale, indeed.

*       *       *

The next morning, I left Ocosingo—henceforward to be known as Ocosingo de Traven—in a three-seater Cessna 300 with Federico Canessi holding the bag containing Traven's ashes. A young TV cameraman was jackknifed in to record the final ceremony from a singularly cramped position. Only a tiny plane could maneuver through the mountains, heavily overcast that day with blue smoke. It was the season when the Indians burned the jungle brush; they were clearing the ground for planting maize before the rains came. Canessi sadly emptied the bag. A bone that had not completely burned knocked sharply against the window on its way earthward. Traven had celebrated the Indians' love for the land, matching it with a strange, hungry love of his own. Now he was part of their lives forever.

Before leaving Mexico, I visited Traven's best friend, Gabriel Figueroa, who was on location shooting the film *Two Mules for Sister Sara*.

"Why," the cinematographer asked me, "is Rosa Elena giving out all these strange stories about Hal's identity?"

"I don't know," I replied. "Perhaps when he died she didn't know what to do except to repeat the information that was on his Mexican passport."

Figueroa looked at me quizzically in his gentle way and said, "Hal must have had twenty passports."

Then, slowly, recalling his years of friendship with the author, he said quietly, "Perhaps, if Rosa Elena continues telling these false stories as the truth about Hal, I will ask her for permission to make a movie about him that is fiction, but it, in fact, will be the truth."

**87**

# Part Four:
# The Novels of B. Traven

**B.** Traven, who predicted that *The Death Ship* would light the horizons with flame, had some advice for the proletarians of the world in his 1931 novel *Government*: apply the good old Bachajontec Indian custom of putting a bonfire under the behinds of your leaders once a year, and above all, never be sentimental! As a novelist, he took his own advice, there were no rules but plenty of bonfires.

What made Traven unique in the '30s and makes him still unique today is his special way of spinning a yarn. At first, a yarn is all that it appears to be. Then, quite unexpectedly, a caustic light is shed on oppressive institutions and the forces that finally drive men to rebellion. His searchlight illuminates the scene with humor both savage and benign. Finally, we see that something precious still remains: the *possibility* of human love and kindness, shining all the brighter with sentimentality stripped away. How fresh he sounds today as he pursues his favorite themes: the corrosive effect of greed and gold on the human spirit; the futility of war; the necessity of rebellion; and the corruption that inevitably follows in a new order.

Whether Traven is writing about homeless sailors, cotton pickers, oil workers, treasure hunters or peons, his targets are always the same: materialist civilization, the state, war, the church and the press. Just as his younger self, Ret Marut, didn't report "news" in *Der Ziegelbrenner* but his own very personal viewpoint, so Traven in his novels has an unorthodox way with his characters. He has a compulsion to digress and he feels free to stop periodically for one of his sardonic sermons on the nature of man, beast and bureaucrat. Sooner or later, the characters catch up with their creator. Indeed, the character very often *is* the creator, particularly in Traven's early work. Gerard Gales, sailor without a passport, is the narrator of *The Death Ship*. He also serves as the voice of Traven in *The Cotton Pickers* (first published as a book under the title of *Der Wobbly*), *The Bridge in the Jungle* (1929) and in many short stories, including "The Night Visitor."

One of the mysteries about Traven's work has been the question of whether he wrote in German or English. All of his books were first published in German, and critics attest to his brilliant use of that language. But after the appearance in 1925 of his first short story, "The Cotton Pickers" (later enlarged to novel length), he insisted that he was an American who knew no German.

The truth is that as an author, he was only at home in the German language, although he could write in English and Spanish.

He claimed that he tried to sell his manuscripts to American publishers first, but that they were rejected. However, the British editions of his books were all translated from the German with the exception of *The White Rose,* published by Robert Hale in 1965. This carries no information about any translation, but I believe it is a heavily—and poorly—edited version of Traven's own English version of the book, first published in Germany in 1929.

*The Bridge in the Jungle,* published in the U.S. by Hill and Wang, came out in Germany in 1929, but oddly, when it was reissued in that country in 1955, carried the notation that it was translated by Werner Preuszer from the "original" American.

When in the '30s American editions were finally published of *The Death Ship, The Treasure of the Sierra Madre* and *The Bridge in the Jungle,* they were "styled" from Traven's own uneven English versions by Bernard Smith, then a Knopf editor.

\*     \*     \*

"It was my wish," Traven wrote to his publisher about *The Death Ship,* "to write a good and entertaining story and I think it is good and entertaining because I have not invented it. . . . If one writes a true story, it is not possible to brood for a long time over the artistic form. One just narrates in the manner one saw and felt it." He expressed a similar thought in the left-wing weekly *Weltbühne* in 1929: "I cannot chew anything out of my pencil, others perhaps can do that, not I. I have to know the people of whom I speak, they must be my friends, companions or my enemies, my neighbors or my fellow citizens. If I want to describe them I have to have seen the things, landscapes and persons before I can bring them to life in my work." Explaining why he lived in an isolated hut in the jungle, miles from civilization, without electricity and under constant attack from mosquitoes, he wrote: "If one wants to become familiar with the bush and the jungle with its life and its songs, its love and its killing, one may not live in the Regis hotel in Mexico City, but must go into the jungle, live with it, love it and marry it. Nothing else will do. . . . Bush and jungle only tell me their stories when I bury myself in them, live all alone in them and with them, ally myself with them unto death and exclude any other friendship. . . . There are people who make a trip through the forest in Thuringen and after their journey is completed can write a jungle or bush novel—these people I call with respect and admiration poets and artists. Since I am neither a poet nor an artist,

I must go into the middle of the jungle or bush if I am to tell a story about it."

*The Death Ship* appeared five years after Ret Marut, hunted for treason, disappeared from Germany. He had fled from Munich to Berlin where his friend Gotz Ohly provided him with a passport and money. Later Ohly received word that the passport had been stolen. There is a possibility that a wealthy shipping owner in Cologne with revolutionary sympathies helped Marut to escape. Despite all the bloodshed and horror Marut had left behind, there is an oddly cheerful good humor—*American* humor—about this story of a friendless sailor stranded in a strange country without seamen's papers or proof of citizenship. That humor is the one totally new note in the writer's voice; it had never appeared in *Der Ziegelbrenner.*

"I can't help it if I see most things in a funny way," Gales says in *The Bridge in the Jungle,* "and if I fail to see fun in supposedly sacred performances or speeches, then I can see only irony in them. . . . I can laugh at a thousand things and situations, even at the brutalities of fascism which as I see them are but a ridiculous cowardice without limits, but I can never laugh at love shown by men for those of their fellow men in pain and sorrow."

*The Death Ship* is an unforgettable novel, at once a devastating attack on government bureaucracy and an ironic but compassionate picture of lost seamen, who have descended into the hell of the S.S. *Yorikke's* stokehold. Like poor Yorick, who was once the king's jester, the *Yorikke* was the bare bones of a ship. Its men, too, were remains of their former selves, men who has lost everything but their ability to work.

As a young actor playing the clowning gravedigger, Marut had heard the lines of Hamlet and marked them well: "Has this fellow no feeling of his business that he sings at gravemaking?" Offstage, Marut continued to sing at gravemaking, derisively attacking those final rituals and hypocrisy with his "death songs" in *Der Ziegelbrenner.* As Traven he approvingly observed that Indians dance at their funeral solemnities: "If it is considered proper to dance at the birth and christening of a child, who against his will is thrust into the pains and sorrows of life, why, in heaven's name should it be improper and heathenish to dance when a person has taken leave of life's persecutions and oppressions and returns to the land of eternal peace?"

Traven's powerful effect in *The Death Ship* is achieved despite his typical weaknesses of erratic structure, awkward language and characters who lack full dimensions. It is as if the author—who didn't want anyone snooping around his past—hesitates to delve even into the lives of the people he creates or reproduces creatively. Gales is memorable despite all that we don't know about him.*

\*      \*      \*

Gales is game for anything; circumstances force him to be. After surviving a shipwreck, he goes on, in *The Cotton Pickers,* to a series of other adventures. For back-breaking work picking a "young mountain of cotton" under the tropical sun, the workers earned all of six centavos; Gales got two more—the magnificent differential for a white skin. His companions were typical of the international fortune hunters who drifted through Mexico in those days with but one thought, to "get rich quick without regard to what happened to the other fellow." Gales feels the misery of the cotton pickers, but he also understands the economic problems faced by Mr. Shine, the American farmer who employs them. Although Shine accuses Gales of being a "bolshie", an "agitator" and a Wobbly, he likes him and gets him a job as an oil driller. Gales' sensitive eye perceives that "in spite of everything ... there is romance in the oil field although at first sight it looks as hopelessly prosaic as a coal mine in the Ruhr." His imagination is captured by the "eternally virgin bush of the tropics with its indefinable mystique, its fantastic secret animal life, its dream-shaped dream-colored plants, its unexplored treasure of stone and metal." He becomes a baker, observes a Mexican strike and philosophizes about robbery, murder and the whores of Tampico. When he drives a thousand head of cattle overland across Mexico, he exults in his freedom and the beauty of the land and gives gentle care to the new-born calves. As he looks at his army of half-wild cattle, he thinks: "Oh, you who took armies of warriors across the Alps to carry murder and pillage into lands of peace, what do you know of the joy, the perfect joy, of leading an army!"

Later, searching for alligators in *The Bridge in the Jungle,* Gales comes upon something more human: a search for a little Mexican

---

*For instance, where did Traven get that name Gales? Is it the English translation of *maruts,* the Sanskrit for storm-clouds? Or did he know about a magazine in Mexico called *Gale's International Monthly for Revolutionary Communism*? It was edited by a goateed American, Linn A. E. Gale, from 1917 until 1921, the same time span in which *Der Ziegelbrenner* existed. There's irony, there's a red herring or another loose thread.

**94**

boy who, less sure-footed than usual in his tight new American shoes, has drowned while racing across a bridge built by an American oil crew. The Indians' attempt to find the boy and the mother's grief build up to the final macabre funeral march when "there came floating through the boiling air the sounds of that musical glory of the century, the great American Te Deum, *Taintgonnarainnomo.*" As Gales ponders the contrast between the ugliness and destruction that civilization has brought to this isolated place and the honest emotions of its people, the author's tone shifts from harshness to tenderness. But he never romanticizes the "noble primitive"; he is much too sensitive to the complexity within every human being to give less than a full measure of it to the Indians. That intuitive perception transcending totally different cultures and languages is what lends greatness to Traven's work. Many critics have said that *Bridge* is his most perfect work of art. Traven agreed. It is also the only one of his books that bears a dedication. The man whose own childhood must have been an ordeal of resentment, questions and confusion about his parents, dedicated the book "to the mothers of every nation, of every people, of every color, of every creed, of all animals and birds, of all creatures alive on earth."

In *The Treasure of the Sierra Madre,* published in 1927 in Berlin, Traven tells an adventurous tale of suspense with "murder lurking all about" as three men hunt for gold: "a very devilish sort of thing" because it "changes your character entirely." In the end, the gold dust is all blown to the wind and only old Howard can laugh at this "joke" that is worthy of the Gods.

*     *     *

As Traven got to know Mexico more intimately, his interest shifted from the foreign adventurers to the Indians and the land itself. On the surface, the lives of the Chiapas Indians—the Tzotziles and Tzeltales, including the Zinacantecans, the Chamulas and the Huistecos—have changed little since Traven wrote about them in his travel book *Land des Fruhlings* (1926). It is a fascinating state, still largely bypassed by tourists, offering a glimpse of another world, another time. The book has not yet been published in English translation.

The conflict that develops when a newer civilization wants to exploit the land for its oil is melodramatically explored in *The White Rose* (1929). It details the maneuvers by which a ruthless American capitalist stops at nothing to secure control of an old hacienda, called Rosa Blanca, for its "black gold." As long as he writes about the Mexicans and their feeling for the soil, Traven is authentic, vivid and moving. But when the scene shifts to C. C. Collins, president of Condor Oil, and his mistress, Basileen, the writing becomes ludicrous and the characters are caricatures. Strangely, despite this, there is a curious fascination about them and they are not totally unsympathetic portraits. Traven is convincing historically, if not dramatically, in his description of how Collins rises to power by manipulating labor unions so that they strike when it serves his interests.

"The bones, sinews and nerves of modern civilization are coal, steel, cotton and wheat," wrote Traven. "He who controls these is mightier than the Lord." He resorted to a biblical analogy of the kind that used to appear frequently in *Der Ziegelbrenner:* "Although no one saw through his [Collins'] plan, it was older than the Bible. To the grievance of many an ambitious merchant of those days, it was a Jew who got the better of the Gentiles and made himself immensely wealthy by stockpiling wheat, until he could dictate a very profitable market price. ... Yes, Chaney C. Collins was greater than Joseph for he was up to date. ..."

For Traven, Collins is "neither more nor less moral if you wish to call it that, than other men. He is honest to himself at times when others are hypocrites, that's all. He is product of his times. He is only one grain of dust swept around the earth in the cosmic storm that seems to whisper, 'Hustle! Or be hustled to death! Devour or be devoured. Don't pity the failures, the devil takes care of the hindmost!' "

With the hacienda finally in his grasp, Collins' sole aim is to pump as much oil as possible out of the earth regardless of the number of people destroyed:

> "As the good Lord in heaven knows very well, an oil
> camp is no kindergarten. There's little room in this world for
> goddamned people who can't look out for themselves. Some
> people are always praying for help from heaven. But we who
> are in oil are different; we're a tough lot, that's what we are.
> And besides, what do men matter? The only thing that
> matters is oil. Yes, OIL. Thank you, Lord, for the flow of
> your infinite bounty. Amen."

*　　*　　*

Where Traven failed to capture the personality of an American capitalist, he succeeded miraculously in evoking the world of men displaced from their land by industrialization and the Diaz dictatorship. His most ambitious project, a series of six jungle novels dealt with the lives of Indian ox-cart (*carreta*) drivers, peons and mahogany. He described the unbelievable brutality of the mahogany *(caoba)* camps: forced into debt and lacking any alternative, the workers were worse off than slaves. The books were published in the German language in the following sequence: *The Carreta,* 1931; *Government,* 1931; *March to Caoba-land,* 1933; *Die Troza* (The Log), 1936 (not published in English, it describes the mahogany industry, and is said to be the weakest of the series); *The Rebellion of the Hanged,* 1936; and *General from the Jungle,* 1940.

These novels contain some of Traven's most tender and lyrical writing as well as his most brutal. Characters are introduced, disappear, and finally emerge again as part of one of the armies that arose all over Mexico to overthrow the dictatorship of General Porfirio Diaz in 1910.

Andrew Ugaldo who learned to read and to think and become a man driving the ox-carts is introduced in *The Carreta.* His love for a poor little Indian girl whom he names Estrellita is sketched with a delicacy and sensitivity that has long gone out of fashion but retains its appeal today. In the love between Andrew and his father, Traven shows once again his poignant response to these Indian parents whose emotions lie too deep for words.

*Government* analyzes with admiring amusement the independent Bachajontec Indian community. These Indians had kept both the church and Diaz' corrupt adminstrators at a distance, democratically electing their own chiefs once a year, inaugurating them literally in the hot seat of public office—and leaving them scarred for life as a reminder of their public service. When one chief tries to stay in office for more than a year, the book rises to a pitch of excitement in a marvelous climactic scene as the Indians move with silent, terrifying swiftness against him.

In *March to Caoba-land,* unlucky young Celso Flores, tricked out of his very hard-earned wedding money, meets up with Andrew in a horrible march through the jungle to slave again in the *monterias.* If they want to survive, Celso advises the new "innocent little lambkins," they must become like *caoba,* "hard as steel," and "get dark red blood" into their veins.

A poor small farmer, Candido Castro, in debt to a doctor who fails to save the life of Candido's wife, joins the others in *The Rebellion of the Hanged,* the most powerful book in the series. At the *monteria* (labor camp), the mahogany cutters are forced to increase their already impossible logging tasks when the three

**97**

Montellano brothers become increasingly desperate about rumors that the dictatorship is falling. (The brothers are supposed to have been modeled on real *monteria* owners whom Traven knew; it may be the reason he didn't return to that part of Mexico for many years.) The workers who can't fulfill their quotas are flogged, hung alive from trees by all four extremities, and left to face the terrors of the fearsome tropical night. Finally, with nothing left to lose, the men rebel; maddened by the tortures inflicted upon them, they ruthlessly kill their oppressors.

Before they can scatter back to their homes, a rebel school teacher, Martin Trinidad, convinces them that they can't be free until the men in all camps are free to have land and liberty. This is the story of *General from the Jungle*. With *tierra y libertad* as their slogan, they form into a rebel army—and find, ironically, after all their isolated battles, that Diaz has long since been overthrown and the victorious generals are already squabbling over the spoils. And so the "muchachos" of the rebel army settle down in their last camp, a fine location for a new village. They call it Solipaz—Sun and Peace.

*     *     *

As Marut, he had called upon men to become "permanent revolutionaries," and that same cry issued forth from Traven in the depths of the jungle. In the title story of *The Night Visitor and Other Stories*, Doc Cranwell expresses the author's theories:

> "Sometimes I think that the trouble with people today is that we don't destroy enough of the things and systems which we believe perfect . . . and make room for absolutely new and different things and systems infinitely more perfect that the ones we destroyed . . . Be like God who destroys with His left hand what He created with His right. . . ."

There is one ultimate purpose for all such change and it is expressed in the same short story through the ghost of an Aztec prince. Here, despite all his irony, cynicism and his relentlessly clear-sighted view of the world, Traven's hope and idealism shine through:

> "For love and nothing but love, man is born into this world . . . Only the love we gave and the love we received in return . . . will be taken into account. In the face of the Everlasting, we will be measured only according to the amount of our love. . . ."

# Part Five:
# A Sampler From the
# Works of B. Traven

# BIRTH AND NATIONALITY

**From** *The Death Ship*

On the first seeing the *Yorikke,* Gales thought, "But, migud, I have never seen a ship like that one. The whole thing was a huge joke. According to international agreements, the name of her home port should have been painted there clearly. Apparently she did not want to betray her birthplace. So you're like me, I thought, without a proper birth certificate. Bedfellows, eh?"

"To Kurt a high official of state had said that his homesickness was only a bum's comedy. A bum cannot be homesick. . . . I was homesick. I am homesick. All my struggling and roaming is but a dope to put to sleep my homesickness. It took me some time, and it cost me thousands of achings of my heart, before I learned in full that this thing which is supposed to be your native land, which God gave to you, and which no one, no emperor and no president, can take away from you, this homeland is today canned and put in files of passport departments and consuls' offices. It is now truly represented only by officials with credentials, by men who have the capacity to destroy your true feeling for your country so thoroughly and so completely that no trace of love for your homeland is left in you. Where is the true country of men? There where nobody molests me, where nobody wants to know who I am, where I come from, where I wish to go, what my opinion is about war, about the Episcopalians, and about the communists, where I am free to do and to believe what I damn please as long as I do not harm the life, the health, and the honestly earned property of anybody else. There and there alone is the country of men that is worth while living for and sweet to die for . . ."

[As their ship sinks, Gales tells Stanislav not to worry about going to heaven.] "In the first place, we have no papers . . . You may think what I say is funny. But why the hell does a man need so many papers here on earth if no one would ask for them up there?" [When Stanislav drowns, Gales wonders:] "How could he have signed on, he had no sailor's card. No papers whatever, they would kick him off right away. . . . [but] the Great Skipper had signed him on. He had taken him without papers ... Can you read what is written above the quarters, Stanislav and Stanislav said, 'Aye, aye, sir. He who enters here will be forever free of pain!'"

## From *The Treasure of the Sierra Madre*

Only the last name was written in the (hotel) register . . . The city had no surplus of officials, and only where there are more officials than are actually needed are people pestered to tell the police all about their private affairs.

## From *The White Rose*

"Jacinto is Margarito's compadre and godfather of some of his children, while Margarito is godfather of Jacinto's two eldest children. Yet, everybody at Rosa Blanca knows that Margarito was more than just that, for without doubt Don Jacinto was Margarito's father. Margarito neither denied nor discussed this. His mother who was still living and busy with the hacienda's hen house as well as general work . . . never said yes or no, for she was neither proud nor ashamed of what anyhow could be of no practical value to anybody. Rosa Blanca never begrudged its flocks of children, those niños who were certainly born in love or they wouldn't have been born at all . . . Don Jacinto naturally cared for them. He didn't need any Civil Court to order him to support orphans on the place. He carried the truest laws in his blood. . . ."

[Of C. C. Collins, the president of Condor Oil Company:] "It wasn't known for certain where he was born, who his parents were, nor whether he'd been to college." When newspapermen queried the famous Mr. Collins on this point: "to each he gave a different, if neat little anecdote."

[At Rosa Blanca, the State Governor suddenly begins to feel like an Indian.] He had talked theoretically to Perez of "home and patria" as defined by law. Legally patria was a definite status which could be expressed by documents depending on civil registers, such as birth and marriage records in state or municipal offices. This legal status is often subject to technicalities, such as a mother's voyage, or family immigration at a certain time. Even a time error in a civil register may cause citizenship and rights of country to be taken from humans to whom those rights belong . . . Here though, the governor began to look at "home" and "patria" in a new way, comprehending that they couldn't be explained by legal regulations . . . the meaning of "home" which he found here was a matter of the soul. The soul itself. For "home" is the germ from which men grow.

**102**

### From *The Rebellion of the Hanged*

[Martin Trinidad, the rebel school teacher, is speaking.] ". . . the first thing we must do is attack the registry and burn the papers, all the papers with seals and signatures—deeds, birth and death and marriage certificates, tax records, everything . . . Then the heirs won't ever come and stick their papers under our noses. Then nobody will know who he is, what he's called, who was his father, and what his father had. We'll be the only heirs because nobody will be able to prove the contrary. What do we want with birth certificates? We live with a woman we love, we give her our children. That's being married. Do we need papers to prove it?"

## GERMANY AND THE GERMANS

### From *The Death Ship*

[Does Gales want to be sent to Germany?] "No, I do not like the Germans. They often go out of their minds without any warning."

"There must be something wrong somewhere, that the police of all the countries I have been in want to ship me off to Germany. The reason may be that everybody wants to help the Germans pay off the reparations, or everybody seems to think that Germany is the freest country in Europe. How can that be with a Socialist president who is more nationalistic than old man Bismarck ever was?"

[Gales was warned by the French that if he didn't leave, he would be deported to Germany.] "I did not like to see the Germans go to war with France again, this time on my behalf. I do not wish to be responsible for another war. It will come anyway."

"I still wonder what the Germans do with their left-overs. I suppose they can them and store them away for the next war. Yes, sir."

"This was the time when in Germany . . . five hundred German shipyard workers would work six weeks under the whip of a Socialist president who had ordered his Socialist secretary of war to break the bones of every German worker who dared strike for better wages. The German labor leaders, having sold every sound principle to satisfy their personal ambition, and having handed over the fate of a new-born republic to unscrupulous financiers . . . had taken already their first successful steps in paving the way for the powerful foes of modern civilization."

### From *General from the Jungle*

[A suggestion is made that Candido Castro, a Tsotsil Indian, find work on the coffee plantations. But Candido doesn't want to go there:] "There are Germans there. They own the coffee plantations. They're crueler than animals in the forest and treat one like a dog. That's impossible. If I went to work on the coffee plantation, I'd kill some German with my machete if I saw him mistreating one of us."

"To have the free and unrestricted disposal of such a large number of ragged, verminous, cowed and totally defenseless prisoners would have rejoiced the heart of the sexually degenerate, spiritually defiled, uniformed invertebrates such as Central Europe produces so cheaply and in such great quantities. Dictators who only feel safe and happy when surrounded solely by slaves are content—for entirely understandable reasons—to rely for acclaim and support on abject minions. With free men capable of feeling even a glimmer of dignity, they wouldn't remain sitting on their thrones a week . . . In modern times, protection comes from the meanest and most miserable henchmen and guardroom parasites, those human dregs, immature and snot-nosed, who because they have no individuality, no spark of personality, can only feel themselves alive because they are permitted to don a uniform cap. These uniform caps transform a human cypher into a semi-being, but as soon as this semi-being is without his uniform cap, he immediately reveals himself for what he really is: an idiotically distorted, crookedly conceived cypher."

## THE CHURCH

### From *The Carreta*

The Catholic Church in Mexico is second to none when it comes to advertising. Again and again you will see on the poor-boxes the following very attractive announcement: "Every centavo you give will be repaid in gold in heaven." A banker who put such a notice in his window would be arrested immediately for obtaining deposits on false pretenses. He would be asked by the judge for positive proof that the deposits would be paid back in heaven and whether or where this heaven was to be found. The Church in Mexico is not asked for proof. It relies on faith. And he who refuses faith blasphemes God. What is an Indian to make of it?

"Better give twice to the church than not at all. Sure is sure."

The Church, this great saviour of souls, had never taught him, nor other Indians who lived in independent communes, the first lesson that saviours of souls and liberators ought to teach: Make the best of your own life first, before you bother about anything else.

The reason why Mexico, a republic of revolutionary character, has hitherto denied the vote to Mexican women, who are not at all inferior to American women in intelligence, is because they know that the Church counts on the women of Mexico to restore its unholy power over the Mexican people, which was broken by the revolution.

### From *The Treasure of the Sierra Madre*

"Bandits are never at a loss about what to do and how to do it. They are well trained in their churches from childhood on. Their churches are filled with paintings and statues representing every possible torture white men, Christians, inquisitors and bishops could think of. These are the proper paintings and statues for churches in a country in which the most powerful church on earth wanted to demonstrate how deep in subjection all human beings can be kept for centuries if there exists no other aim but the enlargement of the splendor and the riches of the rulers. What meaning has the human soul to that branch of this great church? ... They all say an ave maria before killing you, and they will cross you and themselves before and after slaying you in the most cruel way. We wouldn't be any different from them if we had had to live four hundred years under all sorts of tyrannies, superstitions, despotisms, corruptions and perverted religions."

### From *The Cotton Pickers*

I liked to think that perhaps the ghost of an old Aztec priest, unable to rest because of the scores of people he had slaughtered on the altar of his god and whose hearts he had torn from their living bodies to cast at the golden feet of his insatiable idol, had now fled from the bush into the sanctuary of a Christian house to find some repose from his restless wanderings.

### From *The Bridge in the Jungle*

After all, all religion is right and proselytism is wrong.

## THE STATE

### From *The Cotton Pickers*

In all the civilized countries, England, Germany and America and still more elsewhere, it is the police who do the whipping and it is the worker who gets whipped. And then the people who sit complacently at their loaded tables are surprised when someone rocks the table, overturns it and shatters everything to fragments. A bullet wound heals. A cut with a whip never heals. It eats ever more deeply into the flesh, reaches the heart and finally the brain, releasing a cry to make the very earth tremble.

### From *The Death Ship*

"Man's aptness for imitation makes slaves and heroes. If that man yonder is not killed by the whip, then I won't be either. So let him whip. 'Look at that fellow there. My, what a brave guy! He goes straight into the machine gun fire just like that. There is a great man. You are not yellow, are you?' Others do it so I can do it. That's the way wars are fought and death ships run."

### From *Government*

"In civilized Rome it was moral and proper to throw slaves or Christians to the lions in the arena and to enjoy the spectacle; and today it is considered equally right for the State to enroll men in the army against their will, treat them more, or less, humanely, break their will and take away their liberty and throw them into the arena in conflict with the armies of other countries—to murder and be murdered

**106**

for objects which concern the ordinary man as little as the number of spectators and the price of seats concerned the slaves in the arena of Rome. ... king and governments are not unjust because they send their subjects to fight against their will like slaves in the arena, but because they do not raise them above the condition of slaves to be herded without protest into war. This would mean, of course, that the State would be compelled to show such good cause for a war that its subjects would defend their country of their own free will; and all the more willingly the more the decision of their rulers appeared to them to be justified by the needs of their civilization.''

[The four tribes in Pebvil elected a chief to serve for one year only as the head of their federation.] The ceremony by which a new chieftain was instituted in his office was a remarkable one. [The new chief sat with majestic dignity on a low chair woven of wicker-like wood while a pot of glowing charcoal was placed under the hole in the middle of the seat. One of the men gave an explanation in rhyme of the purpose.] He explained in his speech that this fire under the chief's posterior was to remind him that he was not sitting on this seat to rest himself but to work for his people; he was to look alive even though he sat on the chair of office. Further, he was not to forget who had put the fire under him. It was a member of the barrio which appointed the chief for the next year, and it was done to remind him from the outset that he could not cling to office but had to give it up as soon as his time was up, so as to prevent any risk of a lifelong rule or dictatorship which would be injurious to the prosperity of his people. If he tried to cling to his office they would put a fire under him which would be large enough to consume both him and his chair ... The new chief would not forget for weeks what he had had under his seat. It helped him considerably during the first months of his period of office to carry out his duties as his nation expected of him when it elected him. ...

Proletarians would be well advised to adopt this well-approved Indian method of election particularly with the officials of their trade union and political organizations. Not only in Russia, where it is most necessary. In all other European countries too, where Marx and Lenin are set up as saints, the militant working class could achieve success much more surely if they lit a good fire yearly under their leaders' behinds. No leader is indispensable. And the more often leaders were put on red-hot seats, the more lively the political movement would be. Above all things, the proletariat must never be sentimental.

**107**

### From *The Rebellion of the Hanged*

[Martin Trinidad:] "He who rests on his freedom for one moment will lose it in less than a week. I know what I'm saying, comrades, liberty can be lost on the very day you're celebrating it. Don't believe that you'll be free just because your liberty is written in bronze letters and consecrated by law, by the constitution, by whatever you like. Nothing is established for eternity in this world, and all that you can count on is what is renewed and struggled for every day."

## CAPITALISM AND COMMUNISM

### From *The Death Ship*

"If the capitalists would know the truth about Communism, I feel sure they would adopt this system overnight to meet their fear of depressions. Of course, it is by far better they do not accept it; they sure would spoil the whole thing just as much as the original Christian ideas were spoiled the very moment an emperor made them his state religion."

"But even in heaven I should feel sick if I just had to sit around and eat and eat. Slavery results from such treatment. You forget how to work and look after yourself. I should feel unhappy in a Communistic state where the community takes all the risks I want to take myself."

"I do not want to judge. Each age and each country tortures its Christians. That which was tortured yesterday is the powerful church today and a religion in decay tomorrow. The deplorable thing, the most deplorable thing, is that the people who were tortured yesterday, torture today. The communists in Russia are no less despotic than the fascists in Italy or the textile-mill magnates in America. . . . "

### From *Government*

Share pushing is robbery. It is pocket picking. But share-pushing is legally condoned, while picking pockets is punished. Yet in both cases, the incautious are robbed by the man who falls upon them. Speculation in coffee and wheat, whereby the producers lose their land and all else they possess without being able to lift a finger to interfere with this speculation is permitted by law. Stealing a sack of coffee or wheat for the warehouse of the speculator is a serious offense and severely punished. Both the speculation, as also the

**108**

stealing of a sack of coffee, are calculated to damage the victim. In the eye of the law, however, the one is a lawful and proper transaction, the other is robbery. This injustice, or to put it more accurately, this imperfection of the law is a thing we can discuss.

It is all very well to talk of betraying the country and squandering the property of the State. These little deals are mere bagatelle. On the battlefields of Europe, where, according to the belief of excitable citizens the honor and existence of their country are at stake, these deals are only of vaster dimensions. That is the only difference. And it is only that their industrial magnates sell oil, coal, submarines, artillery, warships and armoured plates to foreign powers twice as cheaply as to their beloved fatherland. The conduct of a Mexican general makes such a poor appearance only because it is honest and pursued in the open and because it is concerned with sums which the citizen can encompass. It is only when those deals start at hundreds of millions that there is the possibility, in fact the certainty, of public policy's forbidding an inquiry. For as soon as public policy comes in, publicity goes out and since all concerned, including the judge of the highest court, have their snouts in the same trough, there will be no telling of tales out of school.

### From *The Carreta*

"Where governors, generals, chief constables, diputados, mayors and customs officers rob land and people whenever they have the chance, there is often nothing left for hundreds of unofficial persons but to rob in their turn. When officials steal, it is called corruption: when stealing is unofficial, it is banditry. But you never find bandits except where officials are robbers; and as soon as robbery ceases at the top, the bandits all die out in a week at the bottom."

"Reformers and philanthropists are always a hundred years behind the times. They only follow where the foresight of capital has already led."

"It takes a proletarian, who has less sense than an ox, to believe that he will one day manage a factory or become a member of the board of directors as long as he properly racks his guts and does everything in a hurry to please his drivers. It is therefore an insult to oxen, but not the proletarian, when anyone says: 'You're no better than an ox.' It is the ox who should bring the action for libel.' "

**109**

### From *The General from the Jungle*

"The golden age of the dictatorship had been able to produce an unheard of increase in productivity. But in doing that it had forgotten the human being and the individual and it had also forgotten that each and every thing can be made into a product with one single exception—the brain and the soul of a man."

## REBELLION

### From *The Rebellion of the Hanged*

If the boys had been reasoning men, they would never have rebelled. Uprisings, mutinies, revolutions are always irrational in themselves, because they come to disturb the agreeable somnolence that goes by the names of peace and order ... Those responsible for the acts of the rebels are men who believe it possible to mistreat human beings forever with impunity and not drive them to rebellion.

When the slave begins to be conscious that his life had become like that of animals, that it is in no way better than theirs, it is because the limits have been reached. Then man loses all sense of reason and acts like an animal, like a brute, trying to recover his human dignity.

Ease and speed are not good for revolutionaries ... the real revolution, the one capable of changing the systems, lies in the hearts of true revolutionaries. The sincere revolutionary never thinks of the personal benefit rebellion may bring him.

### From *The Death Ship*

"There are sea-stories and sea-stories, millions of them ... they tell of sailors who are soap-opera singers in disguise ... who have no other worries than their goddamned silly love-affairs. Even that heavenly, that highly praised, that greatest sea-story writer of all time knew how to write well only about brave skippers, dishonored lords, unearthly gentlemen of the sea, and of the ports, the islands and the sea coasts; but the crew is always cowardly, always near mutiny, lazy, rotten, stinking, without any higher ideals or fine ambitions. Of course the crew is that way ... not the skipper, but the sailor is the one who is the first to risk his life."

## From *The General from the Jungle*

They had been treated like childish slaves, who might only open their mouths when spoken to. And in the manner of such slaves, whose chains had suddenly broken, they were now behaving. They had been tortured, beaten, humiliated, struck on the mouth by beasts with human faces. And like beasts, they now set forth to ravage the country and to kill everyone who did not belong to their own kind.

The rebels who now arrived at this ranch did certainly not regard it as their task to ponder that a revolution alone does not alter a system, that it only changes ownership, that only the name of the owner is altered, and that the nation of the State in its role as capitalist may be more brutal, relentless and tyrannical than ever their former masters were. What did systems, old or new, matter to the rebels? They had been so long whipped and hanged, so long humiliated and robbed of free speech, that their community sense, which bound them to their other compatriots from purely natural causes, had been killed. They knew only vengeance and retribution. Destruction was the sole thing they understood.

But rebellions must be if the world is to progress. A lake that has no water flowing through it or is not fiercely agitated by storms soon begins to stink and finally becomes a swamp.

## BROTHERHOOD

### From *The Death Ship*

"Internationalism is just a word that sounds fine from a soap-box. Nobody ever means it; not the Bolshevists either. Stay with your own tribe. Or with your clan. The chiefs need you. If for some reason or other you cannot belong, you are an outcast. You cannot even stay with the dogs of the tribe ... that's why we call ourselves Christians—because we love our neighbors dearly; so let them go to hell or heaven, wherever they want to, so long as they don't try to eat their daily bread with us."

Workers are not at all as chummy toward each other as some people think when they see them marching with red flags to Union Square and getting noisy about a paradise in Russia. Workers might have a big word in all affairs were it not for the middle class ideas they can't shake off.

Stanislav Koslovski got a job on a decent German ship, but they didn't want to take "stinking Polacks". Then he got a third-rater German ship. "But I couldn't stand it," he told Gales. "Workers, and all those what is called 'proletarians of the world unite,' they are more patriotic than the kaiser's generals ever could be, and more narrow-minded than a Methodist preacher's wife. I hardly ever heard anything but: 'Polacks out.' ..."

"Great guys, these fellow-sailors, and sure they are talking all the time about communism and internationalism and eternal brotherhood of the working-class and whatnot. Bunk," I said.

"Now, don't take it this way, Pippip," Stanislav excused them still. "They are educated that way. They can't help it. Was the same with them when war broke out. Karl Marx on their book-shelf, and the guns over their shoulders, marching against the workers of France and Russia. There will still have to pass five hundred years before they won't fall any longer for worn-out slogans. You see, that's why I like it on the *Yorikke*. Here nobody pushes down your throat your nationality. Because nobody has any to play. And don't you think the Russians are so much different. They are as jazzy about their Bolshevik Russia as are the hurrah nationalists of Germany. The Bolshevists shut their doors against hungry workers from the outside as do the American labor unions. Dog eats dog and any devil is a devil for another."

### From *The Cotton Pickers*

The struggle of plants and trees for water is sometimes touching. But when human beings fight over water they surpass all other earthly creatures in their means of combat. Of all creatures man is the most merciless.

It was a new country. Everybody had but one thought and that was to get rich and to get rich quick, without regard to what happened to other people ... They must all exploit something. If they couldn't exploit an oilfield, or a silver mine, or a business clientele, or hotel guests, they would exploit the hunger of the down-at-heel ...

112

There was gold in the veins and muscles of the starving workers as surely as there was gold in the gold mine ... he was more comfortably exploited than any gold mine or oilfield ... Yes, even the bones of a compatriot to whom you extended a helping hand and because of this help, because of over-work, because of the hovels in which he slept, because of the lack of proper nourishment, died of fever and was buried in a pauper's grave, even this could be turned into gold. ... And the foreigners could do it more easily than anyone else, for if non-compatriots made trouble for them they claimed the protection of their legation and freedom-loving America would threaten military intervention.

### From *The White Rose*

Unions exist for a good reason: both capital and labor need them ... When adequately paid and decently treated, this army is eager to fight any system that threatens their liberty to work for capital. In this way, unions are the best mates that capital ever had.

### From *The Treasure of the Sierra Madre*

The discussion about the registration of their claim brought comprehension of their changed standing in life. With every ounce more of gold possessed by them, they left the proletarian class and neared that of the property holders, the well to do middle class. So far they had never had anything of value to protect against thieves ... Those who up to this time had been considered by them as their proletarian brethren were now enemies against whom they had to protect themselves. As long as they had owned nothing of value, they had been slaves of their hungry bellies, slaves to those who had the means to fill their bellies. All this was changed now. They had reached the first step by which man becomes the slave of his property.

### From *The Carreta*

Everywhere on earth the common people take a peculiar delight in cracking each other's heads. For this reason the heads of their masters escape attention. ...

**113**

## EDUCATION

**From *The Carreta***

The Church was not in favor of Indian children going to school. The Church wished the Indian children left in their innocence and ignorance because of such is the kingdom of heaven; whereas once an Indian was educated you could not say where it would end. The case of the Indian, Benito Juarez, was very recent in those days and the memory of it is still fresh today. This Indian of Oaxaca who had remained in blissful ignorance till his 15th year, got the opportunity of being educated and when at last by hard work, he became an educated man, he confiscated the wealth of the church for the benefit of the Mexican people and played havoc with the divine rights which God himself conferred on the Catholic Church in a way that no one had ever dared to do before. No wonder, then, that the church looked askance on education for the Indians.

[Andrew Ugaldo had never seen a railway station, but he knew the word.] Because Andrew knew the word and could write it correctly he felt that he was in some peculiar way familiar with the thing itself ... in spite of its puffing and roaring the monster aroused no fear in him ... And he made the discovery, without being aware whence it came, that if you know of an unfamiliar thing and can call it by its name, this unfamiliar thing loses its power to strike you with alarm. To be able to write this name, besides knowing it, inspired him with unbounded confidence and gave him a sense of his own identity such as he had never had before.

In these few minutes he had an inward experience, trivial in itself, which suddenly opened his eyes to the real meaning of education ... The word, with which he was already acquainted explained and dissected the thing so that there was no mystery left ... His attitude towards education altered completely. He no longer thought of education as being useful only for success and quickness in business. He felt that it had a further value, greater perhaps than its mere business utility ... And so it was the same with Andrew as with all who believe they have struck out a new idea. He believed that education could destroy the threatening and fear-inspiring power of idols, priests and all those dread phantoms of superstition which play off their fooleries on mankind. He thought that if education could render harmless such unknown monsters as the railway, if education could throw down idols and menacing phantoms, it must be able too to set

**114**

his father and all the peons at home on the finca free from the apparently unending oppression of serfdom. He had education and he was free.

### From *Government*

[Andrew explains the meaning of writing to Estrellita.] He wanted to share with her all he possessed, to possess everything in common with her. And he had this wish without knowing that to share knowledge or experience with other men in a spirit of helpfulness makes the giver richer than he was before the distribution of his treasures. For an individual man's treasures of knowledge increase in value as the education and knowledge of those around him increase. The culture of human society does not depend on the exceptional knowledge of individual men surrounded by hundreds of thousands of ignorant and uneducated people; a really high level of culture comes only through the constant interchange of ideas and thoughts between hundreds of thousands of people who are on an equally high level of education and so can make their thoughts and ideas intelligible to each other. For every single person, whatever his race and origin, can once put in the way of it, develop ideas and thoughts which are in their character entirely original and new. When the cultivation of the spirit and the discipline of the intelligence are a privilege of one caste, which makes a closed ring and only deals out its treasures to other privileged persons in small doses, the springs of the human spirit are choked. . . .

To instruct the children of Indians or the Indians themselves and to give them education was accounted a sin against the Almighty. If it had been His will that all men should read and write He would have implanted in them at birth the ability to do so. The will of the Almighty was represented on earth by the Church, whose servants with the aid of supernatural enlightenment, knew very well what God wished and did not wish; for they were in intimate communion with Him as His appointed ministers with full power to enforce His interdicts.

### From "The Night Visitor"

[Gales:] "I had not seen a single book in more than a year. I had hungered for them as a man living in a great city may hunger for green woods, blue lakes, murmuring creeks and cloudless days. . . ."

**115**

[Dr. Cranwell] "I think of books as pillars of the universe."

### From *The Bridge in the Jungle*

[Gales:] "One becomes a philosopher by living among people who are not of his own race and who speak a different language. Experience has taught me that traveling educates only those who can be educated just as well by roaming around their own country ... a trip to a Central American jungle to watch how Indians behave near a bridge won't make you see either the jungle or the bridge or the Indians if you believe that the civilization you were born into is the only one that counts. Go and look around with the idea that everything you learned in school and college is wrong."

"We reach these people [the Indians] so easily with our sailor suits, with our polished shoes and our yeswehavenobananas. Would that we tried once in a while to reach them, not with puffed rice and naked celluloid dames going with the wrong man in the right bed, but with the Gettysburg address, which next to God's rain would be the greatest blessing to all of these so-called republics if we would take the trouble to make the people understand the true meaning of the greatest, finest and most noble poem any American has produced to this day."

### From *The Rebellion of the Hanged*

[Martin Trinidad tells Andrew:] "I'm a school master, a fellow who doesn't know how to crawl or to lick anybody's boots ... I don't know how to bow down or salute those who despise me. Liberty doesn't exist when the expression of thought is forbidden. For you freedom will be the land you cultivate. I don't want land. I want only the freedom to teach what I believe is sensible and true."

### MORALITY ... AND MURDER

### From *The Death Ship*

"Morals are taught and preached not for the sake of heaven, but to assist those people on earth who have everything they need and more to retain their possessions and to help them to accumulate still more. Morals is the butter for those who have no bread."

[Gerald Gales:] "The thought that from now on I should be working with a thief and a murderer day and night, eating from the same dish, perhaps even sleeping in the same bed, this thought did not occur to me. Either I had sunk so low morally that I had lost all feeling for such niceties of civilization, or I had moved so far ahead of my time and so far above the moral standards of the day that I understood every human action, and neither took to myself the right to condemn nor indulged in the cheap sentimentality of pity. For pity is also a condemnation even if it is not recognized, even if it is unconscious. Should I have felt a horror of Antonio, a revulsion against shaking him by the hand? There are so many thieves and murderers about with diamonds on their fingers and fat pearls in their cravats or gold stars on their epaulettes ... Every class has its thieves and murderers. Those of my class are hanged; the others are invited to the President's ball ..."

### From *The Cotton Pickers*

"What is murder? I thought. It all comes to the same thing. The law of the jungle. The whole world was a jungle. Eat or be eaten! The fly by the spider, the spider by the bird, the bird by the snake, the snake by the coyote, the coyote by the tarantula, the tarantula by the bird, the bird by .... So it went round and round. Until there came a world disaster, or a revolution and the whole circle would begin again— only the other way round ... It's the way of the jungle. You pick it up so quickly in the bush. It's all around you and after all, civilization is only the natural outcome of an outstanding capacity for imitation."

Honor remains upright only if you don't have to starve; for a sense of honor depends on the number of meals a day you have, how many you would like to have and how many you do not have. There are therefore, three categories and three different conceptions of honor.

### From *Government*

A murder committed by a civilized Mexican is in the eyes of the law the same murder as when committed by an Indian who has no resemblance whatever to a civilized Mexican in his soul, his feelings or his economic conditions ... The caballero can only continue to live if he has killed the man who has sullied his honor or 'if he cannot kill him, he prefers to be killed himself. It is no satisfaction to him that a judge, who regards this insult as a common occurrence, punishes

**117**

it with a fine or four weeks imprisonment. This attitude of the caballero is a primitive one. Perhaps. But so is the feeling of one mature nation that another has insulted it. Yet highly civilized peoples still go to war. So long as they do that, the apparently incomprehensible murder committed by an Indian cannot be judged by an outsider.

## LOVE

### From *The Cotton Pickers*

Those [prostitutes] at the top of the profession spoke not only fluent French, but were also conversant with English, Spanish and German. Certain forms of entertainment are pleasurable only if accompanied by the music of the mother tongue. And certain sensations come to full flowering only if they are aroused by words that strike a certain chord which a foreign language can never touch. For such words bring back the memory of the first feeling of shame, thoughts of the first girl you desired, and sensations of those mysterious hours which ushered in the first feeling of maturity. The mistresses of the art were well aware of this. And that was why the ignoramuses who knew only one language did not get on; they would always be centavo peddlers in the darkest parts of the quarter ... But you would search in vain for the romantic figure of Goethe's bayadère.* Time is money. And for sweet trifling, for tender playfulness, for hours of longing and groping towards fulfillment these mistresses of the art lack what has been called the love of the adored woman ... What was lacking was the sweet longing for the lover. This confirms the priceless value of the loved woman.

## INVISIBLE LIFE

### From *The Death Ship*

"The *Yorikke* has taught me another big thing for which I am grateful.

---

*A bayadère (from the Portuguese *bailadeira*, "dancer") was a female temple dancer in India. The reference is to Goethe's ballad *Der Gott und die Bajadere* (The God and the Bayadère).

She taught me to see the soul in apparently lifeless objects. Before I shipped on the *Yorikke,* I never thought that a thing like a burned match or a scrap of paper in the mud or a fallen leaf or a rusty worthless nail might have a soul."

[Stanislav asked] "How come you say 'Gracious Lady' to the winch?" ... "I wanted to tell him that many things apparently lifeless have really souls like humans and that you have to treat them accordingly."

"When old salts start to spin, all the rattling and crackling of a windjammer ceases. The ship gets quiet so as not to lose a single word of the story. All the sea-stories I know have been told to me by ships, not by people, and the stories written by pensioned skippers are the bunk. I have seen ships chuckling on Sunday afternoons when the crew was sitting on the deck telling stories of the seven seas and cracking jokes about skippers and mates and chiefs. I have seen ships cry and weep when stories were told of brave sailors who had gone to the bottom after having saved a child or another fellow ... the ship is always on the side of the crew and never takes the part of the skipper ... a crew may leave a ship; their stories never leave ... Suppose the crew mutinies—the ship immediately joins them ... I knew a ship that went out with a crew of strike-breakers. She was still in sight of the coast, less than 12 miles off, when she went down, just to drown that gang."

### From *March to Monteria*

This was the very earth which conceived caoba, gave birth to caoba and developed caoba to its full splendor, vitality and strength. For this aristocratic timber can attain its beauty, its full consistency and its hardness only where it has to fight cruelly and pitilessly for its existence and survival. Whatever is conceived here, and once conceived grows and survives has to be of truely heroic nature. Softness and timidity are stamped into the mud to rot. The one that loses the battle serves as fertilizer for the one of greater beauty, strength and nobility."

### From *The White Rose*

In the farthest corner, leaning against the adobe wall that enclosed the patio and yard, lay an old wheel of an ancient carreta, no living

**119**

person could recall. The wheel was dry and silvery with age, but it had been cunningly made from mountain oak, good for years yet, maybe a century, before the termites could eat it up. Little boys had climbed through it like snakes, older boys stretched out on it to tell bloody battle yarns, it had seen courtships on moonlight nights ... and there it was, the old carreta wheel, peaceful, tenacious, wise in its own proud value, dreaming over its long history, still firm in silvery grey wood, stoically awaiting the day when nature would be done with it ... The wheel would stay. For it was not merely an inanimate object, not just a piece of patina-ed wood, but much more: a symbol. A symbol of the race the peopled the republic, a race that was and ever will be the same. A race that can't be moved. That outwits time and endures.

## From *The Cotton Pickers*

" ... The sun stays mighty and dignified in the universe. It is a god, it is the only god, the redeemer, the savior, the only visible one, the always present, the ever young, the ever smiling god, forever an exulting song of eternal creation. It is the creator, the maintainer, the begetter and the producer. It gives and wastes at the same time, never ceases to bless the earth with fruit and beauty, yet never asks for prayers or worship, nor for thanks. And it never threatens punishments."

"I could gaze over that jungle for hours on end. There wasn't a minute's rest in the eternal battle for survival, for love. Creation and destruction ... a tropical jungle is so rich with life that you simply cannot become desolate if you feel the whole universe in every little insect, in every lizard, in every bird's chirp, in every rustle of the leaves, in every shape and color of flower."

[Gales has been hired to drive a thousand head of half-wild cattle 350 miles overland.] To man, who for as long as we know has always been a diurnal creature, there is something indescribably uncanny about the tropical night. ... Even the giant herds begin to get restless as soon as the sun has gone down ... Clear as only the tropic night can be, the blue-black sky arched over the singing prairie. The glitter-ing stars studded the velvet night with gold. And the stars shot here and there, hundreds, thousands of them, as if they had come down from the high dome of heaven to seek love and give love, then to return to the still, lonely heights where no bridge spanned the void from one to the other. The glow-worms were the only visible life down here. But invisible life sang with a million voices and made music with violin, flute and harp, with cymbal and bell. And there lay my herd. One black, dark shape next to the other. Lowing, breathing and exhaling a full, warm heavy fragrance of natural well-being, so rich in its quiet earthiness, such balm to the spirit, bringing with it such utter contentment.

My army! My proud army which I had led over river and mountain, which I had protected and guarded, which I had fed and watered, whose quarrels I had settled and whose ills I had cured, which I had sung to sleep night after night, for which I had grieved and worried, for whose safety I had trembled and whose care had robbed me of sleep, for which I have wept when one was lost, which I had loved and loved, yes, loved, as if it had been my own flesh and blood! Oh, you who took armies of warriors across the Alps to carry murder and pillage into lands of peace, what do you know of the joy, the perfect joy, of leading an army!

## AN ENTIRELY NEW WORLD

### From "The Night Visitor"

[Dr. Cranwell:] "Sometimes I think that the trouble with people today is that we don't destroy enough of the things and systems which we believe perfect ... and by destroying them make room for absolutely new and different things and systems infinitely more perfect than the ones we destroyed ... Be like God who destroys with His left hand what He created with His right ... As far as I'm concerned, I am convinced that the world would likely be a hundred times better place to live in today if mankind had a chance now and then to discard all tradition and history and start fresh with no worn-out ideas, platitudes and opinions to hamper the birth of an entirely new world."

# Selected Bibliography

*Works by B. Traven*

IN ENGLISH

*The Bridge in the Jungle.* New York: Alfred A. Knopf, 1938; Hill and Wang, 1966.

*The Carreta.* London: Chatto & Windus, 1935. New York: Hill and Wang, 1970.

*The Cotton Pickers.* London: Robert Hale, 1956. New York: Hill and Wang, 1969.

*The Creation of the Sun and the Moon.* New York: Hill and Wang, 1968.

*The Death Ship: The Story of an American Sailor.* New York: Alfred A. Knopf, 1934; Collier Books, 1962.

*The General from the Jungle.* London: Robert Hale Limited, 1954. New York: Hill and Wang, 1973.

*Government.* London: Robert Hale, 1935. New York: Hill and Wang, 1975.

*The Kidnapped Saint and Other Stories.* New York: Lawrence Hill and Company, 1975.

*The March to Caobaland.* London: Robert Hale Limited, 1961. (As *March to the Monteria.*) New York: Hill and Wang, 1971.

*The Night Visitor and Other Stories.* New York: Hill and Wang, 1966.

*The Rebellion of the Hanged.* New York, Alfred A. Knopf, 1952; Hill and Wang, 1972.

*Stories by the Man Nobody Knows.* Evanston, Ill.: Regency Books, 1961.

*The Treasure of the Sierra Madre.* New York: Alfred A. Knopf, 1935; Hill and Wang, 1967.

*The White Rose.* London: Robert Hale, 1965.

## SELECTED BIBLIOGRAPHY

IN GERMAN

*Das Totenschiff: Die Geschichte eines amerikanischen Seemanns.* Berlin: Büchergilde Gutenberg, 1926.

*Der Wobbly (Die Baumwollpflucker).* Berlin/Leipzig: Buchmeister-Verlag, 1926.

*Die Baumwollpflücker (Der Wobbly).* Berlin/Leipzig: Buchmeister-Verlag, 1929.

*Der Schatz der Sierra Madre.* Berlin: Büchergilde Gutenberg, 1927.

*Der Busch.* Berlin: Büchergilde Gutenberg, 1930.

*Der Banditendoktor (Der Busch).* Frankfurt a.M. Hamburg: Fischer-Bucherei, 1955.

*Land des Frühlings.* Berlin: Büchergilde Gutenberg, 1929.

*Die Brücke im Dschungel.* Berlin: Büchergilde Gutenberg, 1929.

*Die Weisse Rose.* Berlin: Büchergilde Gutenberg, 1929.

*Der Karren.* Berlin: Büchergilde Gutenberg, 1931.

*Die Carreta (Der Karren)* Berlin: Universitas-Verlag, 1953.

*Regierung.* Berlin: Büchergilde Gutenberg, 1931.

*Der Marsch ins Reich der Caoba: Ein Kriegsmarsch.* Zurich, Wien, Prag: Büchergilde Gutenberg, 1933.

*Caoba.* Hamburg: W. Kruger, 1950.

*Der Marsch ins Reich der Caoba.* Berlin: Volk und Welt, 1954.

*Die Troza.* Zurich, Prag: Büchergilde Gutenberg, 1936.

*Trozas (Die Troza).* Berlin: Volk und Welt, 1954.

*Rebellion der Gehenkten.* Zurich, Prag: Büchergilde Gutenberg, 1936.

*Ein General kommt aus dem Dschungel.* Amsterdam: A. de Lange, 1940.

*Sonnen-Schöpfung.* Zurich, Wien, Prag: Büchergilde Gutenberg, 1936.

*Macario: Eine Novellette.* Zurich: Büchergilde Gutenberg, 1950.

*Der dritte Gast.* Frankfurt a. M.: Europaische Verlags-Anstalt, 1958.

*Aslan Norval.* Wien, Munchen, Basel, Desch-Verlag, 1960.

*Una Canasta de Cuentos Mexicanos. (Ein Korb Mexikanisher Erzählungen.)* Mexico, D.F.: Compania General de Ediciones, August 1956.

**124**

## Works by Ret Marut

*Der fremde Soldat.* Novellette. In: "Marz". Marz-Verlag, Berlin/Munchen; 9. Jg. (1915), Heft 42, S. 50-54.

*Nebel.* Novellette. In: "Marz". 10. Jg. (1916), Heft 27, S. 14 bis 17.

*Die Klosterfrau.* Novelle. In: "Westermanns Monatshefte." 62 (1918): 689-98.

*Der Ziegelbrenner.* Leipzig: Edition Leipzig, 1967.

## Works by Richard Maurhut

*An das Fraulein von S . . .* Novelle. Munchen: Verlag J. Mermet, 1916.

## Works on Traven

Baumann, Michael L. *B. Traven, An Introduction.* University of New Mexico Press, Albuquerque, 1976.

Chankin, Donald O. *Anonymity and Death: The Fiction of B. Traven.* The Pennsylvania State University Press, 1975.

Fallen de Droog, Ernst "Travens Tod." *Der Monat.* No. 228, Vol. 19 (September 1967).

George, Manfred. "B. Traven's Identity." *New Republic,* March 24, 1947.

Graf, Oskar Maria. *Prisoners All!* New York: Alfred A. Knopf, 1928.

Hagemann, E. R. "A Checklist of the Work of B. Traven and the Critical Estimates and Biographical Essays on Him; together with a Brief Biography." *Papers of the Bibliographical Society of America* 53 (first quarter, 1959).

Hanley, James. "Sugi-Mugi." *The Spectator,* January 26, 1934.

Hays, H. R. "The Importance of B. Traven." *Chimera* 4, No. 4 (1946).

Heidemann, Gerd. "Das Ratsel Traven gelost." *Stern,* August 25, 1963.

——— , "Er ist ein Sohn des Kaisers." April 13, 1969.

——— , "Wer ist der Mann, der Traven heist?" May 7, 1967.

Humphrey, Charles Robert. "B. Traven: An Examination of the Controversy over His Identity with an Analysis of His Major Work and his Place in Literature." Ph.D. dissertation University of Texas, 1965.

Johnson, William Weber. "Who is Bruno Traven?" *Life,* March 10, 1947.

——— , "The Traven Case." *New York Times Book Review,* April 17, 1966.

——— , "A Noted Novelist Dies in Obscurity." *Los Angeles Times Calendar,* April 13, 1969.

**125**

———— , "Pilgrimage to the Sierra Madre." *Life International,* May 30, 1969.

Langford, Walter M. *The Mexican Novel Comes of Age.* Notre Dame and London: University of Notre Dame Press, 1971.

Miller, Charles H. Introduction to *The Night Visitor and Other Stories by B. Traven.* New York: Hill & Wang, 1966.

———— , "Our Great Neglected Wobbly." *Michigan Quarterly Review,* June 1967.

———— , "B. Traven, Pure Proletarian Writer." In *Proletarian Writers of the Thirties,* edited by David Madden. Carbondale and Edwardsville: Southern Illinois University Press, 1968.

Miller, Charles H. and R. E. Lujan, eds. "B. Traven, A Special Section." *Texas Quarterly* 6, No. 4 (1963).

Recknagel, Rolf. *B. Traven: Beiträge zur Biografie.* Leipzig: Verlag Philipp Reclam, 1966, 2d ed., rev. 1971.

Raskin, Jonah. "B. Traven: Writer from the Jungle." *University Review* 31 (October 1973).

Schmid, Max (Gerald Gale) "Der Geheimnisvolle B. Traven." *Tages-Anzeiger* (Zurich) November 2, 1963–January 4, 1964.

———— , Introduction, Epilogue to *Khundar.* Egnach, Switzerland: Clou Verlag, 1963.

Smith, Bernard. "B(ashful) Traven." *New York Times Book Review,* November 22, 1970.

Spota, Luis, "Manana Descubre la Identidad de B. Traven." *Manana,* August 7, 1948.

Suarez, Luis. "Al Borde del Fin, Traven Penso En un Escopetazo al Estilo Hemingway. *Siempre!* April 9, 1969.

———— , *"Siempre!* Desentrana, al Fin, La Misteriosa Actividad de Traven en La Selva de Chiapas." *Siempre!* May 7, 1969.

———— , *"Siempre!* Revela, al Fin, El Misterio Literario Mas Apasionante Del Siglo y Presenta al Mundo a B. Traven!" *Siempre!* October 19, 1966.

———— , "Traven y *Siempre!* Una Polemica en Europa!" *Siempre!* November 16, 1966.

West, Anthony, "The Great Traven Mystery." *New Yorker,* July 22, 1967.

Wieder, Josef. "B. Traven und Ret Marut." *Die Kultur,* February 1960.

Whitney, Dwight. "More About Traven." *Life,* February 21, 1948.

*Other Works Consulted*

Aaron, Daniel. *Writers on the Left.* New York: Harcourt, Brace and World, 1961.

Arendt, Hannah. "The Jew as Pariah." *Jewish Social Studies,* April 1944.

Balfour, Michael. *The Kaiser and His Times.* Boston: Houghton Mifflin.

Bang, Herman. *Denied a Country.* Translated by M. Busch and A. G. Chater. New York: Alfred A. Knopf, 1927.

Buber, Martin. *Between Man and Man.* Translated by Ronald Smith. London: Kegan Paul, 1947.

Carroll, John, ed. *Max Stirner: The Ego and His Own.* New York: Harper & Row, 1971.

Fishman, Sterling. "Prophets, Poets and Priests." Ph.D. thesis, University of Wisconsin, 1960.

Guzman, Martin Luis. *The Eagle and the Serpent.* Garden City, L.I.: Dolphin Books, Doubleday & Company 1965.

Heiden, Konrad. *Der Fuehrer.* Boston: Houghton Mifflin Co.

Horowitz, Irving Louis, ed. *The Anarchists.* New York: Dell Publishing, 1964.

Landauer, Carl. "Bavarian Problems, Part I," *Journal of Modern History* 16 (June 1944).

Liptzin, Solomon. *Germany's Stepchildren.* Cleveland and New York: World Publishing Company, 1961.

Mitchell, Allan. *Revolution in Bavaria: The Eisner Regime and the Soviet Repubic.* Princeton, N.J.: Princeton University Press, 1965.

Nettl, J. P. *Rosa Luxemborg.* London: Oxford University Press, 1966.

Reed, John. *Insurgent Mexico.* New York and London: D. Appleton & Company, 1914.

Ruhle, Jurgen. *Literature and Revolution.* New York, Washington and London, 1969.

*The Rigveda Sanhita,* translated from original Sanskrit. London: H. Wilson, 1850.

Sachar, Abram Leon. *A History of the Jews.* New York: Alfred A. Knopf, 1965.

Schoenberner, Franz. *Confessions of a European Intellectual.* New York: The Macmillan Company. 1946.

## SELECTED BIBLIOGRAPHY

Shirer, William L. *The Rise and Fall of the Third Reich.* New York: Simon and Schuster, 1960.

Tannenbaum, Frank. *Mexico: The Struggle for Peace and Bread.* New York: Alfred A. Knopf, 1950.

——— , *The Mexican Agrarian Revolution.* New York: Macmillan, 1929.

Tuchman, Barbara. *The Proud Tower.* New York: Macmillan, 1962.

Turner, John Kenneth. *Barbarous Mexico.* Austin and London: University of Texas Press, 1969.

Toller, Ernst. *Look Through the Bars: Letters from Prison, Poems, and a new version of the Swallow Book.* New York, Farrar and Rinehart, 1937.

——— , *I Was a German.* New York: William Morrow.

Ullstein, Herman. *The Rise and Fall of the House of Ullstein.* New York: Simon and Schuster, 1943.